D1608721

Hunting the
QUAILS
OF NORTH AMERICA

C·SMITH

BEN O. WILLIAMS

ILLUSTRATIONS BY CHRISTOPHER SMITH

Hunting the QUAILS of North America

Ben O. Williams

ILLUSTRATIONS BY CHRISTOPHER SMITH

WILLOW CREEK PRESS

MINOCQUA, WISCONSIN

DEDICATION

For my grandchildren, Andy Baker, River and Kessly Lovec

Published by Willow Creek Press
P.O. Box 147, Minocqua, Wisconsin 54548

For information on other Willow Creek titles,
call 1-800-850-9453

Designed by R.S.K. Book Design

Library of Congress Cataloging-in-Publication Data
Williams, Ben O.
    Hunting the quails of North America / by Ben O. Williams ; illustrations by Christopher Smith.
    p. cm.
    ISBN 1-57223-307-9 (hardcover : alk. paper)
    Includes bibliographical references
    1. Quail shooting—North America. 2. Quails—North America. I. Title.
    SK325.Q2 W56 2001
    799.2'4627--dc21   2001003715

Printed in Canada

TABLE OF CONTENTS

ACKNOWLEDGMENTS

I should like to express my gratitude to all the folks who gracefully shared their fine birds, dogs and hunting experiences with me. Ben Brown, Dale and Lila Critz, Jim Fergus, David Foster Drummond and Seth Hadley, Wendell Holeman, Gerald Malzac, Billy Morris, John Nash, Tom Petrie, Leigh Perkins, Dick Schulze, Steve Smith, Bill Sprague, Dave Zalunardo and many others for being hunting partners and photo models. A special thanks to the wildlife biologists working for state or federal agencies, universities, private institutions, research stations and organizations like Quail Unlimited. They are the foundation and the cutting edge of wildlife preservation and for maintaining our hunting heritage. Every dollar spent researching wildlife, preserving and reestablishing quail habitat not only benefits today's outdoor person but also generations to come.

FOREWORD

by Jim Fergus

The first time I ever hunted with Ben Williams was a few years ago in his home-country of Montana. I was with my friend, the writer, Rick Bass, and we were both like a couple of awestruck kids at the opportunity to make a hunt with Williams. You see, in the world of bird hunting, getting an invitation to hunt with the legendary Ben Williams and his equally-storied Brittany's is a little like being invited to play a round of golf with Tiger Woods, hit a few tennis balls with Pete Sampras, or toss a football with John Elway. I don't know if mere mortals ever actually get to do those things, but if they do, one thing is for sure: they're going to learn something.

As for me and Bass, it's true that two bigger hackers have never lived. Oh, sure, we've both written books ostensibly about bird hunting, but those who have been afield with us know that that fact doesn't necessarily translate into competency. For my part, I've always enjoyed hunting with Rick, because he's one of the only guys in America whom, on any given day in the field, I have an even chance of out-shooting. And I figured if I shot badly in front of Ben Williams, Bass would likely shoot as badly, possibly even worse. Not that I would ever wish my friend a bad day of shooting, but as all poor shots know, there's something tremendously comforting about having someone else to miss with.

Before the hunt we stopped off at the ranch house to visit with the landowner whose property we were hunting. It's what Ben Williams refers to in these pages as "kicking gravel." But in this case, the rancher (who I will call Gerard, although that isn't his real name) was an old friend of Ben's, a second generation Montanan whose parents had immigrated from France in 1908 to homestead this land. Many of their early neighbors couldn't make a go of it here, the 160 acres allotted by the Homestead Act clearly inadequate to make a living in these spare prairie hills. But Gerard's family hung on, proving up on the abandoned claims until they owned a good-sized piece of ground. Ben told us that in the old days, missing most of all their national libation, Gerard's parents used to have railroad cars full of grapes shipped in with which to make their own wine.

Unlike the gigantic modern trophy ranches of Montana's nouveau gentry, the ranch house was a modest affair, a simple clapboard cottage set in the cottonwoods on the creek bottom. Someday a movie person or perhaps a Silicon Valley billionaire will probably buy this ranch, and build a 20,000 square foot house on the top of a hill, with a spectacular 360-degree panoramic view of the surrounding mountain ranges, and with a vast expanse of gleaming metal roof that looks like it might contain an entire shopping mall beneath it. But right now, the place was just as it should be and always had been, the last of the "real" working cattle ranches, settled by real working people. The living room was full of well-worn, distinctly unstylish furniture, probably purchased from the Sears-Roebuck catalogue many years ago, and the kitchen was warm and smelled of nearly a century of cooking.

Ben always brought some cigars for Gerard, although the old man probably shouldn't have been smoking anymore at his age. But what the hell. He had been born on the ranch, had lived here all his life; two weeks earlier his wife of over fifty years had died quite unexpectedly, and now Gerard seemed grateful for the company, not to mention the cigars. An ancient ranch dog lay by the front door, wheezing and snuffling in his sleep, and in the corner of the room stood an American flag and an American Legion flag side by side.

Gerard was a gentle, soft-spoken old fellow and we talked about this and that — the cattle business, the weather, the terrible winter of '48-'49; he told us that they had raised sheep on the ranch for the war effort during World War II and he asked where we were from and where we were headed, genuinely interested. Although we had obviously come here to hunt, Ben Williams made no fast move to excuse us, which was just fine with us. Sitting in Gerard's living room, kicking gravel was the kind of experience that is being sadly lost in this day of destination lodges and paid hunting preserves that cater strictly to sportsmen

and exist largely outside the true fabric of rural life.

But finally we said good-bye, thanking Gerard for allowing us to hunt on his place. Then we drove up into the hills above the ranch house, into the classic short-grass prairie, an endless reach of rolling highlands never turned by the plow and covered in native grasses, yellow in the late fall, and dusted with a powder of fresh snow. There were easier places to hunt on the ranch for sure, down lower on the edges of wheat fields for instance, where the Huns liked to feed, and in the CRP fields that adjoined them where both Huns and sharp-tailed grouse took advantage of the good cover to loaf during the day. But I think that Ben was saving those birds for some of his less-fit flatlander friends, because say what you like about my and Bass' shooting skills, one thing we can both do is walk. So today we were going after what Ben referred to as his "prairie birds," the coveys that largely shun the easy living afforded by agriculture in favor of the natural life in the native grasslands.

I maintain that Ben Williams knows more about prairie game bird species than any other human being on the planet. A school teacher in Livingston for many years, Williams got to know all of the ranching families in the area, taught most of their children, and gained hard-earned hunting access to hundreds of thousands of acres of private lands, not to mention millions of acres of Montana's public lands. He hunts his dogs almost every day during the season, and runs them virtually every day in the off-season, locating coveys, checking nests, making bird counts. Ben Williams has hunted so many days in his lifetime, shot so many birds, that these days he is more apt to carry a camera in the field than a shotgun, as he was on this day. And he is far more interested in the habits, habitats and life-cycles of the game birds, what he calls, "learning wild things," than he is in filling limits.

So now we were walking the hills together, watching the dogs work the country, making large casts, sometimes appearing on distant hilltops, other times down in the bottoms. As most readers of this book may already know, Williams raises a nationally-famous line of Brittanys, breeding a larger, sturdier, stronger, bigger-running version than is typical of the breed—dogs that can hunt the big prairie country all day long. And while he might have five or six dogs on the ground at once, hunting with Ben Williams and his dogs is an oddly relaxed experience; there is no yelling, little whistling; Ben and his dogs seem to communicate on some quiet, private, mutual-respect level.

I remember the first point of that day, three of Ben's dogs, Hersh, Clyde and Winston, locked up like ice sculptures on the top of a hill, the Absaroka mountain range already white on the horizon, the fields and meadows lying dormant in the fall below. Bass and I started to hurry over to the dogs but Ben said, gently, "I never run to a point. It makes the dogs nervous. And it makes the birds nervous, too." So we walked at a leisurely pace down the hill and up the other side, walking up straight behind and past the dogs who remained staunchly on point, joined now by their confederates, Ripper, Tierra, and Pat, all backing.

Ben was behind us with his camera and on the covey rise, true to form, Bass and I both whiffed—one, two, three, four times. But Ben Williams didn't care. Let's face it, the man has seen it all; it's conceivable that he's seen even worse shots than us. "We're out here to have a good time," he said, "the dogs are here to have a good time, and I don't care

what happens. Let's go get 'em, boys."

Now, with this book, I'm delighted to see that Ben Williams has turned the considerable force of his and his dogs' attention, their hunting skills and collective knowledge about upland game birds to the American quail species. As readers will learn early in these pages, Williams began his long and distinguished upland bird hunting career pursuing bobwhites as a boy on his family's farm in Illinois with "Mike the Dog." From these humble beginnings, he has gone on to hunt all the different species of quail all over North America, with hundreds of stellar dogs across the years. Like all of Ben Williams' work, and like the man himself, this book is a charming, relaxed, straight-forward, knowledgeable, plain-spoken, often funny, never pedantic, and always-honest account of his experiences along the way.

Since that first Montana hunt, I have also been lucky enough to hunt desert quail with Williams in southern Arizona, a hunt that appears in these pages. What all of us who have been afield with Williams have learned, and what comes through loud and clear in this book, beyond, of course, the man's vast wealth of knowledge and experience in the natural world, is Ben Williams' great spirit of generosity. And if he fudges the details occasionally on the written page, it is only to make his hunting companions perform a bit better in the re-telling than they actually have in the field. Miss ten shots and make one, and Williams will make you feel like the greatest wing shot on earth.

Similarly, while it's true that on any given day Ben's elite fleet of vastly more experienced hunting dogs are going to find 90 percent of the birds and make 90 percent of the points, as they had on this day, he'll even make your dog feel a little better about herself. I remember after the hunt that day in Sycamore Canyon, driving back down a desert two-track, tired dogs in their boxes, Ben Williams at the wheel of his truck; we were both sipping cold beers from the cooler as the sun set over the distant mountains. "You know, Jim," Ben Williams said, "your dog did just great today. What a great little dog!"

Jim Fergus is the author of
A Hunter's Road and *A Thousand White Women*

INTRODUCTION

To me there is something very special about bird hunting.
But this book is not only about hunting game birds, bird dogs
and bird guns, even through they have been an important part
of my life. It's also about each bird's origin, distribution,
life cycle, behavior, habitat, food and daily routine.
These I call, Learning Wild Things. My essays are about
hunting wild things and wild places with clouds
moving overhead and rocks beneath my boots.

Chapter One
BOBWHITE QUAIL

Today, I have a maze of equipment, a kennel full of pointing dogs and a complex
upland bird hunting schedule, as do many of my hunting partners. But as a boy, I have
pleasant memories of the simplicity of hunting the uplands for game birds. Paper shot-shells,
a single-barrel shotgun and a dog was all I needed. Work, school and hunting clothes
were one and the same and I could be ready to go afield at the drop of a hat.

ILLINOIS: QUAIL IN MY BACKYARD

The Place: The bobwhite quail (*Colinus virginianus*) is native to Illinois and shares the game bird hunting season with pheasants and mourning doves. In the 1940s, Illinois' quail season started in November and continued into January. Hunting varied within this season depending upon the depth of snow. Central Illinois is the northern fringe of good bobwhite quail country.

Farther north where I lived bird numbers were seldom outstanding and fluctuated each year from fair to poor depending on the seasonal weather. On weekends after my chores were done I went quail and pheasant hunting.

I would scan the ice box, then the pantry looking for last night's leftovers to take along. No luck! But a look was worth it, for mother was a great cook and to have a slice of her apple pie or perhaps a chunk of her dark chocolate cake for lunch was special. I would make a peanut butter and jelly sandwich, wrap it in wax paper first, then newspaper. I would carefully place the sandwich in my shirt pocket, opposite the shoulder I mounted the gun. I once wore one of my shirts that had only a right-side pocket and mounting the gun over a lump added to the difficulty of shooting bobwhites bursting into the sky. After shooting several rounds, the recoil from the gun against a packed peanut butter and jelly sandwich made it lose some of its appeal, though the dog didn't seem to mind.

Dogs in my life have been the most important part of bird hunting.

Next I would go to the bedroom, stuff shotgun shells in the front pockets of my blue jeans and take the Stevens single-barrel .410 shotgun from the corner of the room behind the door. Downstairs, I would race the dog out the door. Several large outbuildings blocked the full view of the grassy meadow that merged into the cornfield 100 yards from the house. A large fenced vegetable garden was cut out of the hayfield. Keeping the garden was supposed to be a family chore. The instructions were to keep the garden well manicured with black earth showing between each row of vegetables. Of course, there were times when my brothers and sisters pitched in and helped. But at times it seemed I was the sole custodian of the garden other than the chickens, songbirds, pheasants, cottontail rabbits and an occasional covey of quail. Needless to say, the grounds were not weed-free.

Beneath my rubber boots, the tall golden timothy grass lay horizontal, crushed by an earlier snowstorm. I passed the harvested garden and walked the shocked cornfield's muddy edge. Bordering three sides of the cornfield were wide, overgrown, unplowed strips of various kinds of brushy hardwoods, forbs and grasses. Down the middle of each strip was a dilapidated wood and wire fence that followed the property line. The meadow, the garden and the cornfield were about 12 acres—my back yard. Even though the acreage was small, all of it was bobwhite quail-friendly and to a young boy anything larger than a baseball diamond seems big. At the end of the cornfield, beyond the run-down fence were weedy crop fields and big woods. Running through the center of it were weed-choked spur-line railroad tracks. This was my wilderness playground.

In the late summer, looking for game birds, fishing or hiking along the never ending railroad tracks took priority over exposing the black earth of the garden to the sky. By the time school started, the unattended cornfield would have less black earth exposed than the vegetable garden. The weeds along the fences were higher than a six-foot ladder, and the weekly train pulling from one to three cars plus a caboose seemed to tunnel through a canopy of vegetation. It was difficult hunting, but good for quail.

I broke through the heavy cover and came out on the tracks. The dog, of course, was someplace in the cornfield chasing rabbits. I called but he didn't come.

The Dog: My brothers and I had an untrained springer spaniel by the name of "Mike, the Dog." During the day, mother insisted the dog be outside, but anytime one of us grabbed a shotgun, the dog came out from one of his many hiding places in the house and joined the

No one is ever quite ready when a covey of bobwhite quail flushes.

activities. I've had a great number of pointing dogs since, and looking back I believe he may have been a liability hunting bobwhite quail. He found quail coveys, but most of the time, flushed the birds out of shooting range into the heavy cover. Mike's approach to working a scattered covey of quail in high, thick cover was the same as running ringneck pheasants—get 'em up as fast as you can. When he smelled birds, he jumped in the cover, running around in circles flushing quail in all directions. Once in a while I would get a shot at a fast-flying object going through a chokecherry or hazelnut patch, but the decline of the quail population in Northern Illinois had nothing to do with Mike and me.

After several loud calls, sometimes it worked. Once, I heard Mike crashing through the brush toward the railroad tracks. I saw him coming, but he didn't stop. He crossed the tracks behind me and hunted the cover to my right. It seemed I walked miles down the tracks and I knew the bobwhite numbers were down.

Up until then I had had no luck. I'd been daydreaming about catching smallmouth bass. Finally I realized the dog was working something. A covey of bobwhites flushed at the far edge of the railroad bed and three birds sailed across in front of me. I shot and then watched them fly along a fence line into heavy cover and disappear out of sight, Mike in hot pursuit.

Mike had three specialties: chasing rabbits; chasing pheasants; and chasing any other quarry that runs. "Mike the Dog" had heart, desire and a great place to hunt, but no formal training. What he did best was try to please his hunting partner. His retrieving was restricted to an occasional mourning dove that'd been pot shot, lying dead under a telephone high line, or an unlucky rooster pheasant that flew into my shot pattern. A .410 single barrel, full choke shotgun may be okay for shooting cottontail rabbits, but for a young boy bobwhite quail definitely have the advantage.

In my late teens, I set aside my favorite gun, hung up my tattered hunting coat and said goodbye to my bird dog. The Korean War (Conflict) interrupted bird hunting. Instead of being drafted, I joined the United States Navy.

At sea, letters sometimes took months. Word came from home. "Mike the Dog" had passed away. The letter brought vivid memories of hunting together. On the ship that day, the wake transformed into railroad tracks. I saw Mike flushing a covey of bobwhite quail. I saw myself bring the muzzle of the .410 shotgun up, heard the loud report and saw him retrieving a fat bobwhite quail to me.

Each time I call out Mike's name I live this moment. He always did his job to the best of his ability, but I'm not sure I always did mine. My companion and first hunting dog may not have been the best, but the fond memories endure. Over the years I've owned three pointing dogs by the name of Mike, all good hunters in their own right and all named after "Mike the Dog."

UNFAMILIAR COUNTRY

The Contact: I had a plan. After the Korean War, I returned to Illinois and enrolled for the fall semester at Northern Illinois University. Being absent for five years left me without a bird dog, hunting clothes or a gun that fit. Getting the hunting gear was easy. In the 1950s, buying a used shotgun at a hardware store in the Midwest, you had two choices, 12-gauge automatics or pumps. In pheasant country, smaller gauges, over-and-unders, and side-by-side shotguns were not thought of as pheasant guns. The 16-gauge shotgun was still popular in Europe but had practically disappeared from the North American hunting scene. Stores had rows of 12-bore shotguns and one or two unpopular 16-bores.

I was looking around for a gun, but not seriously. A used Ithaca 16-gauge pump action, modified choke caught my eye. The 16-gauge was a compromise, lighter than a 12-gauge, but it certainly packed plenty of punch for pheasants and was fast enough for quail. It was built for hunting all kinds of game birds and light enough as a walking man's gun. Because it was an odd bore, the price was right. One disadvantage to this gun was that not all stores carried that size ammunition. The gun wasn't new, but it was clean and fit fairly well, so I bought it.

Even today I recommend the 16-gauge to anyone who's hunting different kinds of game birds. I've killed a lot of birds with that gun. But over the years I found other shotguns that fit better and have a faster swing for shooting quail.

August 15: I was driving a yellow '51 Chevy convertible, attempting to follow an old county road map with my finger and the gravel road with my eyes. Outsiders consider this once tallgrass prairie monotonous, a land of nothing but fallow fields and standing corn. For the unhurried, though, section-line roads—grids I called them—were the way to see the landscape. Ten-foot-high green corn was divided by a narrow gravel road. Both sides of the road had a wide, grassy barrow pit and brush-lined

wire fence locking in the corn. After each mile I slowed down. The road was only visible straight ahead, but curved wheel ruts indicated an intersection. First I turned right, then left, zigzagging from west to north. Beyond every turn young pheasants were present, chasing insects along the dusty gravel. They were in no hurry as I drove by.

At noon, I was waiting for the Texaco station attendant to fill the gas tank of my car. DeKalb, Illinois, is a small, quiet farming community known nationally for its DeKalb hybrid corn. But to me it was a pheasant hunting paradise. The attendant cleaned the dust off the windows. I paid him $3.25 for the gas and asked about living quarters. The attendant handed me the local newspaper and said, "This time of year there's all kinds of housing available."

By sundown, I was settling in, thinking about looking for a place to hunt and a hunting companion. Hunting season was less than three months away. Yet without a bird dog it wasn't the same. I had read that English pointers and English setters historically have been the most popular pointing breeds for the upland hunter. I had never owned a pointer and it seemed to me the English setter was best for pheasant country.

Next morning, I was drinking coffee and reading the morning newspaper. An ad caught my attention. "Two year old English setter to give away. Call after five." The ad excited me. I could hardly wait until five o'clock. As a bird hunter, that phone call may have been the best I ever made. A man answered the phone. I explained my interest in the English setter for bird hunting.

"Sir," he said, "we've had second thoughts about giving the dog away. I've never hunted the dog, it's our pet and the family has decided to keep him." He apologized, but informed me that west of town on Highway 30 a man had a kennel full of dogs. He thought some looked like setters.

I headed right over. I introduced myself to the elderly gentlemen who answered the door, then added I was a new student who just moved to town, heard he raised English setters and was interested in buying one.

"Sorry son, I don't raise setters, but I do have pointing dogs." Disappointed, I was about to leave when he asked if I'd like to see them. I hesitated, but for some reason I said yes. I went along just to see what kind of dogs he had, but my thoughts were still focused on an English setter. He opened the first kennel gate and called out "Mike!" several times. A beautiful, long-legged orange and white dog ran

Bobwhite quail and double guns go together.

to him, put his front paws on the man's chest and wagged his short tail. The dog was magnificent.

"What kind of a dog is it?" I asked.

"He's a Brittany spaniel, a pointing breed from Brittany, France." Mr. Oberlin proudly said, "When the war ended I was one of the first to bring them to United States. They're great dogs."

Mike came to me and jumped up, his hazel eyes sparkling with enthusiasm. He wagged his tail, jumped down and ran toward the house.

"May I see the others?"

Mr. Oberlin turned to me — he could see I liked dogs — and said, "You look older than most beginning students. Were you in the military?"

"Yes sir, spent four years in the Navy."

"How do you plan on keeping a dog while you're in college?"

I told him I wasn't sure, but I'd find a way.

He smiled and asked if I planned on getting a part-time job.

"I get the GI bill, but I also plan to work some," I said.

"How would you like to come and work for me? You can work whatever hours you want. I'm retired, travel a lot and need someone to take care of the dogs when I'm gone. And you could also work the dogs.

"A young man by the name of Bill Johnson had been helping me, but he graduated and got a teaching job in southern Illinois. He told me the teaching job doesn't pay well, but it's good bobwhite quail country. He's a good lad, has a way with dogs. I gave him a young bitch that he trained. She runs big, should make a great quail dog. I may go down and hunt with Bill this fall and see how the dog is doing."

"Sir, I don't know anything about training dogs," I answered.

"Neither did he when he started," Mr. Oberlin stated. "With Brittanys you don't have to. All you have to do is take them out and run 'em. The dogs do the rest. I run dogs and hunt just about every place in this county, and you can too, if you help me. I'll see to that.

"Now, about buying a dog. If you work here you won't need a dog. You can hunt one or two of mine. And if you stay, I'll give you a couple of pups when you graduate," Walter Oberlin said with a big grin.

Oberlin's kennel had about 50 dogs. I jumped at the job.

Bernie, a yellow Lab owned by Leigh Perkins, is a bobwhite specialist and works off a mule-drawn wagon at May's Pond Plantation.

The Hunt: I arrived at Bill Johnson's place. Isolated snow patches glistened in the bright sun. The morning was cold—shooting glove weather. Bill, who had taken advantage of this year's good quail hunting in southern Illinois, invited me down.

Walter Oberlin had been Bill's guest for the past week. Obie had excellent shooting and his dogs did extremely well. Walter, a born shooter, had a keen eye for killing birds and an inherent ability as a dog breeder, but he never bragged about either.

After Obie's quail hunting trip, he told me that quail hunting brings out the best in dogs and men. He complained that running pheasants were tough on pointing dogs, and if he were young, he'd move to quail country. Obie said Bill Johnson's young female Brittany gained more experience hunting quail in one week than his dogs could hunting the whole pheasant season.

I just listened.

The first point came as Bill and I emerged from the end of a shocked cornfield. Only the Brittanys' white and orange heads were visible. We hurried up the gentle slope of the rolling terrain, reached the crest of the hill and stopped a moment to catch our breaths. The dogs, now in full view, stood out like whitewashed stones, out of place in windblown leaves from the yellow-green osage-orange balls that littered the ground.

Several steps behind the rigid pointers Bill split left and walked past the trailing dog. I went right, walking slowly, gun ready, ahead of the lead dog, but nothing happened. First I walked around kicking the ground looking for the quail and stopped at the edge of an overgrown, brushy windbreak. Then I turned 180 degrees, looking back at the two motionless Brittanys. The closest dog rolled its eyes, telling me the birds were there. Three bobwhites buzzed out from the brush behind me. Hearing the sound, I spun around, muzzle of the gun straight up over my head, hoping more birds would flush.

At that moment Bill touched off a shot toward the heavy cover and both dogs catapulted into motion looking for a downed bird. Nothing fell. We looked at each other, mouths open. Bill knew this covey by their first names and said to me, "Ben, only three birds got up. Last week the covey had over fifteen. Something must have broken them up. Perhaps a Coopers hawk. The rest of the covey has to be here." Bill suggested we split up.

Bill followed his Britt, Sally, upwind along the

windbreak. I called my dog, a young roan male by the name Pepper, and he followed me through the tangle of osage-orange trees. I carefully sidestepped the maze of green balls under the black-barked trees and hunted the opposite side of the windbreak, walking parallel to Bill. For a moment I could hear Bill's dog crashing through the brush. Ahead of me, Bill was looking for the rest of the covey. I was looking for the three birds that flushed.

Pepper half pointed and a single flushed from under a fallen orange tree. No fault of the young dog. I raised the gun, but it was too late to shoot. I followed the tree line. The Brittany, unsure of himself, made short casts. I heard two shots, then Bill's low voice calling to Sally. "Hunt dead, hunt dead, hunt dead."

I walked around the end of the windbreak, then toward Bill. He was holding a cock bobwhite in his hand. His Brittany sitting alongside him had another in her mouth. "Nice shooting," I said. Bill stroked Sally and took the other male quail gently from the dog's mouth. He held the pair in one hand, looking down at them for some time, then slipped them into his vest. Bill said nothing, but Bill never talked after killing a bird.

We walked across the cut field toward the windbreak on the other side. I broke the silence, calling Pepper to "whoa." Seconds later, Pepper was alongside Sally. Both dogs were locked up on point. I told Bill that Pepper is a young dog and needs more work backing other dogs. Bill nodded in agreement. I stopped and watched the two dogs, rock solid, on point. For a moment I thought, there is far more thrill in watching a pointing dog than there is in hunting over a flushing breed.

We passed silently by the rigid dogs. Gun up, I was ready, my heart beating fast. Wide-eyed, I sensed the energy of the dogs waiting for the flush. In seconds everything became blurred in motion—dogs, man, gun and birds. The essence of hunting over pointing dogs is in the anticipation of the flush; the moment of climax is the gun's report whether one kills a bird or not. The covey escaped, twisting and turning through the jungle of trees. Both dogs crashed through the understory, then returned birdless.

Midday we rested the two dogs and ourselves. We ate lunch, talked about dogs, dog work, the number of birds we missed and the few we killed. By early afternoon, the dogs pointed two large coveys and did a great job working several singles. Bill killed a couple more birds. In the afternoon I did the same.

We called it quits, not taking advantage of the best time of day for hunting, when the birds are feeding and moving about. I had a long drive home and Route 47 should be driven while it's light. Fall was fading fast, the vivid oak leaves were gone.

Heading north the signs of winter became more evident. The tires were whistling. The car was whipping the tallgrass along the side of the road, the telephone poles became blurs and the golden harvest fields blended together. The countryside looked birdy and driving a blue highway, with a dog at my side, I had time to think about the day's hunt. The car was moving, but time seemed to stand still.

The Move: Farms in the 1940s and '50s were family operated and changed little. Extensive land use for crops and livestock was nonexistent. Country roads were gravel, the sides and barrow pits uncut. Shelterbelts, small fields, wide fence rows, unused corners and wetlands were all part of the landscape. The environment was wildlife-friendly.

With the Korean conflict over, much of the Midwest was still superb for pheasant hunting. Bobwhite quail along their northern range were holding on by a thread. Then the 1960s arrived, farming practices changed and rapid population growth in many areas occurred, having a detrimental affect on suitable habitat for wildlife. This was the beginning of the decline of good bird hunting in Illinois.

After graduation, both my wife Bobbie and I taught school for one year in a small town in northern Illinois. Across the Mississippi River the Midwest sea of grass swept thousands of miles westward to the sagebrush flats and foothills of the Rocky Mountain front. There the land lifts sharply up through steep forested sides to lofty peaks, then swings down the western slopes to the bright blue water of the Pacific Ocean. It was time to go west.

West: I believe one matures faster serving a hitch in the military. I'm sure that's true aboard ship. A ship runs and stays afloat from the maturity and teamwork of the crew. Everyone works together, from the captain to the seamen. Maturity and teamwork is also the glue that bonds a bird dog and a bird hunter together.

I have the background to keep a ship afloat. Walter Oberlin, owner of Oberlin's Kennels in DeKalb, Illinois, presented me with the opportunity, the knowledge and a gift of a lifetime of how man and dog share the hunting experience.

After working with Walter Oberlin's dogs, I gradually select-bred the dogs for hunting the big open prairie. I didn't do yard drills with the dogs. Everything was done at the dogs' leisure in the big open spaces and always on wild game birds. When pups were four or five months I took them with the self-trained dogs. The pup learned from the other dogs. When a pup learned he couldn't catch the birds, he watched the other dogs and started to self-break. I'm very strong on natural field training and letting the dog use its natural hunting ability. Let the dog be a dog.

To me, of all the animals, bird dogs, more specifically the pointing breeds are the most interesting. No man can learn all the complexities or behavior of a pointing dog and every dog's personality is different, but with an open mind, deep interest, maturity, companionship and teamwork, both man and dog become better hunters. After five decades, my kennels are still full. Today I have 12 Brittanys, two English pointers and one English setter—some old, some young, but all good hunters. After all these years, each day is different in the field and the dogs and I are still learning. I don't consider myself a professional dog trainer, but a breeder involved in improving a pointing dog breed for hunting western game birds.

KNOWING THE BIRD

Bobwhite Quail Origins and Distribution: The bobwhite thrived long before the European settlers arrived, even though the bird's numbers were small. They were never fully dependent on the forest being opened or the prairie being turned over by the plow, but this greatly extended and improved the bobwhite's habitat. It was not until the encroachment of civilization to the south and west that the bobwhite quail increased greatly and also extended its range.

The bobwhite quail once had a wider distribution than the other five species of quail indigenous to North America combined. At one time, bobwhites were found throughout the eastern, southern, midwestern United States and Central America. If a line was drawn starting from the coast of southern New Hampshire due west though the Great Lakes to the center of South Dakota, turning due south to the south Texas line, it would be this eastern portion of the United States that is the natural range of the bobwhite quail. This area covers over half of the United States but not all of it had a stable population. The north and west lines

are irregular at the edges, having a fluctuating population of birds depending on weather conditions. At one time bobwhites lived in 35 contiguous states. These prolific birds were also introduced in several states where they were not originally found. Today Oregon, Washington and Idaho have a few isolated areas of bobwhites. Except for a few limited places in Canada and northeastern Mexico, the bobwhite quail range lies within the United States borders.

Early increases of bobwhite quail in the southeast were due to habitat enhancement. Virgin forests were cleared, creating small farms with openings for cultivated crops. One man could work only so much cropland, so fields were small, and edges wide with lots of weedy cover. Today this is called sloppy farming, but it's good bobwhite habitat. Also, the first stages of plant succession from cutover piney woods produced an abundance of quail for short periods of time.

By the mid-1800s, the most desirable land in the interior for farming had been settled. This land-use change in the midwestern states greatly influenced the bobwhite quail population. Not only were forests cleared for agricultural lands, but miles and miles of tallgrass prairie and mixed prairie were broken for subsistence farming.

Approximate range of bobwhite quail.
There are many gaps within the present range having no birds
because of human activity and loss of habitat.

Bobwhite quail once had a wider distribution than all of the other five species of quail indigenous to North America.

Most farms were small, having a quarter- or half-section of land (a section of land is one square mile, 640 acres) with different fields and crops surrounded by fenced-in edges. Dirt and gravel lanes followed section lines to individual farms, creating diversified cover on both sides of the roads. Hedgerows, windbreaks and rock walls dotted the countryside.

The peak bobwhite distribution encompassed some 850 million acres of land, but within this same area lived 80 percent of the people of the United States. In general, this range with good cover had relatively high levels of bobwhites. After World War II, farming practices changed and the human population exploded. For the past five decades bobwhite quail have gradually declined and in general the trend is still downward. Wild bobwhite quail still can be hunted in many states, but the gaps within these states having no quail or quail habitat are enormous.

Today wild bobwhite quail may have less available living space than any North American gallinaceous bird other than the prairie chicken and sage grouse. Said in another way, the bobwhite quail probably has lost more ground or usable habitat than any game bird in the last 20 years and it is still happening on a grand scale.

The reasons are simple—high human density, clean crop farming, intensive grazing by cattle, more green cut meadows and other land-use practices that reduce or eliminate flora. In the South, woodlands have diminished and pasture development and cattle-raising have largely replaced row-crop farming. In the North, hedgerows have been eliminated and cover has become more sparse.

The decline of the bobwhite is related to one thing — habitat. In the long term, a decrease in any game bird's population is not from annual fluctuations, predation or hunting pressure, but the deterioration of habitat changing the birds' environment. Even though some of the land where the bobwhite quail once lived is gone, much of it can still be restored. Today the key to better quail hunting is to regenerate bobwhite quail habitat wherever possible.

IN THE BUSH, IN THE HAND

The bobwhite quail, known throughout North America, has numerous recognized subspecies, sometimes called races, or varieties, including the masked bobwhite, (*C. v. ridgwayi*) of Arizona. However, the subspecies masked bobwhite is remarkably different in color. Masked bobwhite is not addressed in this book. Except for a few wildlife biologists, no one knows much about the bird. The masked bobwhite's range is very limited, it has no hunting season and is possibly on the verge of extinction.

The name bobwhite comes from the bird's distinctive call. As a young boy, walking to and from school, the familiar cheery sound "bob-WHITE! bob-bob-WHITE!" filled the meadows and brushy fence rows. Not many days after the first whistle, spring becomes evident, awakening the foliage and flowers, changing the landscape of muted browns to multiple greens.

In years past, the Eastern outdoorsman did not have to journey far for excellent bobwhite hunting. Other species of quail in North America were of little concern to him. For the Southerner, bird hunting meant quail hunting. These folks referred to bobwhites as southern quail, native quail, swamp quail, or partridge, depending upon where they lived.

Once the great populations of quail in the East declined, the quail hunter looked elsewhere to hunt upland game birds. Hunting different species of quail in the West grew in popularity and eastern colloquial names like "quail" or "partridge" were rarely used. Today, the name bobwhite or bobwhite quail identifies this bird across the nation.

The bobwhite is a plump-bodied bird, our smallest quail, and other than the dove it is the lightest in weight of all the upland game birds in North America. A close second is the Gambel's quail of the Southwest. A big male bobwhite tops the scales at 6 ounces, is 11 inches in length, and has a wingspan of 15 inches. The female is lighter in weight and slightly smaller.

Male and female bobwhite are very different in color, but similar in appearance. In different areas of the birds' large range, both sexes have slight color variations. The male bobwhite's most conspicuous mark is a white eye-stripe that extends from the bill to the nape of the neck. The white is bordered by dark brown. The top of the head and neck are brownish-black. The bird's back, breast, rump, tail and wings are mostly brown, with some mottling of mixed light and darker browns. The underparts of the male have scaled markings of white and dark brown. The flanks have three rows of white feathers edged in black, creating stripes. The eye, bill, legs and feet are gray-black.

The female's plumage is like the male's except her throat and eye stripe are a buff light yellow instead of white and the borders are light brown instead of dark brown. The markings and coloring of her body are almost identical to the male's. Her coloring overall is a bit lighter than the male.

The male bobwhite's whistle has always been a welcome sound. The call "bob-WHITE" is heard primarily in the spring and early summer, possibly proclaiming a territory or seeking the attention of a mate. Both adult sexes have calls to alert their young of danger and to inform them of their location. Young birds keep in touch with each other by uttering low sounds as they feed and move about. When a covey is scattered the adults have calls to communicate with the young and to assemble the group back together. Numbers mean safety, so little time is wasted regrouping.

LIFE CYCLE AND BEHAVIOR

At the first signs of spring, the covey slowly breaks up and pairing begins. It is not certain whether the male or female establishes a territory. A territory is a small unit of land with suitable habitat for the pair to raise their young. The male defends this territory and drives off other males. Bobwhite start nesting several weeks after pairing, but weather also determines the time of nesting. If spring is late, birds stay in a covey longer, or if already paired they may temporarily covey up again during cold weather.

After pairing, nest building begins. A shallow depression is scratched in the ground by one or both adults, then lined with dried grass. Nests are well concealed with a grassy canopy. Nests are located in weedy fence rows, brushy field corners, woods, thickets and other places with good nesting cover. During egg laying, the nest is unattended. The hen will normally deposit an egg a day. Once the clutch of 14 to 16 eggs is completed, the adults begin the incubation period. Both the male and female sit on the nest. Rarely, a male will incubate a clutch of eggs if the female is on another nest, or absent for other reasons. Females also have been known to lay one or more eggs in another nest.

If the nest is destroyed by a predator, humans or severe weather conditions, the female will attempt to nest again. If the second nest fails, many times the hen will nest until successful. Unlike game birds that have collective breeding grounds, called *leks*, paired birds spread out their nesting times over a longer period of time. Birds hatching over a longer time frame have a greater chance of survival due do to better weather conditions and more cover.

Bobwhite quail were originally thought to be monogamous, but recent studies from radio-marked birds show evidence of some birds being ambisexual-polygamous. (Both female and male incubate and raise broods, but usually with the same mate during the breeding season). Extra-pair breeding is evident in most ambisexual-polygamous species; however, it is not documented in wild bobwhite quail populations. The studies also indicate that only a limited number of male and female bobwhites are ambisexual-polygamous. It is thought that some birds remain paired for life, even though their lifespan is quite short, but this depends on numerous factors such as loss of nest or broods.

The eggs hatch within a few hours of each other after incubating for 3½ weeks. After the last chick hatches, the adults and brood leave the nesting site. The adults emit a variety of sounds to keep the young close by. The male and female will search out openings and likely places for the young to catch insects and find other food. Good habitat and warm weather are important factors for young bird survival. During the first two weeks of a quail's life insects are an important food source because they are high in the protein needed for rapid growth.

Chicks have voracious appetites and within a couple of weeks, the young birds are eating not only insects, but berries, fruits and seeds. Life becomes easier for the young birds in midsummer and fall, as food is plentiful both in variety and abundance. Each covey has a small home base, such as a thicket, within a much larger area, but this sizable space will also have overlapping coveys, especially in feeding areas.

By later summer, the bobwhite has many choices of foods. About 90 percent of the bobwhite's diet consists of vegetable matter. The rest is animal matter, consisting of anything that moves, from grasshoppers to plant lice. Most of the vegetable matter that bobwhites consume is seeds. Quail prefer a great variety of small seeds and much of it is found in agricultural lands. Bobwhites also eat a great variety of greens when available. They will eat almost every part of various green plants.

At 16 weeks, the juveniles are full grown, strong flyers resembling their parents. Family units break up in late summer and early fall. This is a time of disoriented movement for young birds. Before the quail hunting seasons starts juveniles will begin to intermix with neighboring broods, and it is not uncommon to see groups of 20 birds together. This period has been called the "fall shuffle" and can last until early winter. Shifts are determined by the birds' habits, food and cover. Shifts are also a means of relocating within the range that offers protection and food in winter. These movements are short distances. Some coveys spend several days in one place and then in another within a small area, especially if there is a division such as a road in their home ground.

The normal range of a covey of bobwhite is about a quarter of a mile, but birds of neighboring coveys will intermix. Even though a covey is tied to a small area, single birds that join another covey may travel much farther. A small minority of birds have been recorded several miles from their original covey, but most mixing occurs in less than a square mile.

Most hunters think of a covey as a family group, but during the summer months adults with few chicks will join a larger group within the same range. Unsuccessful breeding pairs also will join a covey. Two small coveys that share the same feeding grounds often combine. In fall, groups of quail of various ages may be found together. The interchange of birds among coveys continues throughout the hunting season. If a single covey is shot down to low numbers they will join another group. Small groups band together. Usually small coveys that combined during the fall will stay together throughout the winter.

Weather conditions are the primary factor for maintaining good numbers of birds going into the fall season as with most game birds, but this is especially true with bobwhite quail. As cold weather approaches, large groups divide, forming smaller coveys of ten to 15 birds in their winter homes. In spring, coveys are often larger than at any other season but seldom stay together for long periods. There is also evidence that very few birds of a covey occupy the same home range from year to year because of neighboring coveys intermixing. Quail depend on numbers for survival. More eyes and more ears are helpful. If an enemy takes one bird the group still survives.

BEHAVIOR IN DIFFERENT GEOGRAPHICAL LOCATIONS

Compared to most game birds the bobwhite's world is small. The bird does not migrate but does have some restrictive seasonal movements. After surviving the rigors of winter, the bobwhite population as a whole is at its lowest level.

Nesting time for bobwhites is fairly well-defined but varies considerably, the difference being partly regional and partly seasonal. In the birds' southern range, breakup of coveys begins early and nesting may begin in April and can last until October. In the Deep South there have been reports of birds nesting as late as November, but the most

favorable conditions for hatching occur between June and August. Hatching peaks occur several times during the nesting season. Re-nesting attempts can be numerous due to weather conditions, predation and other uncontrollable factors. Studies have shown a pair of quail may raise more than one brood during a breeding season in the Deep South.

In the birds' northern range, covey breakup is much later as are nesting and hatching. The hatching period in the North is much shorter, due a shorter growing season. The habits of the bobwhite, like those of many other game birds with a large distribution, vary considerably. Also in the north country, cover, winter temperatures, snow conditions and excessive rain in the spring diminish nesting success. In the northern states, more than one brood per season is unlikely, or extremely rare, due to the fact that the breeding season is much shorter.

Severe winters can limit entire quail populations and move the inhabited range several hundred miles south. The opposite can happen if several mild winters occur in succession. With warms springs, quail return to their northern fringe if good cover exists. Climate not only limits the geographic distribution of the species but affects its local abundance as well.

The western edge of the bobwhite's range is always in question. The farther west one goes, the drier the climate and the less woodland cover. Quail populations in this environment occasionally have high numbers, but these high numbers are confined to ideal habitat, and in a dry environment ideal habitat is restricted to riparian areas.

The southeastern range is characterized by mixed piney woods and farmlands, both ideal for good quail production as long as quality habitat is maintained. The quail plantations are within this range. Quail plantations are areas exclusively managed for bobwhite quail hunting and, in some years, have the best quail shooting in the country. Unfortunately most of it is private and restricted to the lucky few.

Today, the mid-continental prairie is the heartland of the bobwhite country in the United States. Where once the tallgrass prairies merged with the mixed prairies, the earth is rich, generally fertile and agriculture is the way of life. Woodlands are scarce in some portions of this range, but for the most part the country is laced with waterways and numerous brushy draws and hillsides. The south-central area's climate is moderate, with fairly humid summers and warm winters, but summer rains are important for good bird populations.

HABITAT

Every game bird species has different habits, even those living in the same location. The bobwhite quail has a particular way of living, and knowledge of the birds' habits and habitat is important to everyone who hunts them. The more you know about a species of game bird the more success you will have in the field.

The habitat of all species of quail are less complex than you may think. Bobwhite need two kinds of cover: grassy and woody shrub habitat. Bobwhite require diverse cover just as they need diverse food sources. An ideal cover would have weeds, brush piles, fence rows, small areas of bare ground and a canopy of overhanging cover. Bobwhite also need dense cover and small stands of trees or thickets to escape from predators. Intermingled vegetation with different plant species break up the spacing, and add different heights to the cover, forming more edges.

Places that come together are called edges. Quail like edges! The more edges within a covey's range, the safer it is for the birds to move about. This arrangement can come in many forms. Woodlands and brushy fence rows around edges of grainsfields, tobacco fields, cotton fields, fallows fields and CRP fields (Conservation Reserve Program) are used year-round by quail for feeding, resting, dusting, loafing and roosting. Grasslands, including pastures, fringes of prairie grasses, hayfields and roadsides are used in spring and summer for nesting, roosting in good weather and feeding. Brushy cover of briars, windbreaks, thickets, sagebrush and other shrubs are used in fall, winter, and spring for roosting, escape cover and feeding. Woodlands, hardwoods, softwoods, cutover, and riparian bottomlands are used year round for roosting, escape and feeding. In the quails' southeastern range, large blocks of well-managed grassy, open pine forest or savannas are home to many bobwhites. But if you look carefully, these areas are also edges within edges.

For example, if a covey of young birds are feeding in the edge of a soybean field, within a few feet of a thicket, and a shadow appears in the sky, in less than a split second the birds can be under an overhead canopy. Food and protective cover are within the same edge. If the quail are farther out in the field, they will not have any overhead cover for protection.

Quail tend to stick closer to the edges of the field to feed where they have access to cover. Centers of large open fields are never used even if the best food source is there. Areas that are weedy, with abundant food and cover are ideal for quail to feed. Edges and corners of uncut crop fields left for the birds are also choice places for birds to feed.

Shelter, too, is essential. The birds' wide range, north to south and east to west, has many different climates and kinds of habitat, which have an effect on quail populations. But of the different habitats in the bird's range quail must have different types of cover for their daily and seasonal needs. The bobwhite requires sufficient shelter for protection against heat, cold, storms and predators, but the cover and food have to be as close together as possible. The arrangement of cover types and the proportion are also important to maintain a healthy population of birds.

Bobwhite quail do not wander aimlessly from place to place, but establish a cruising radius, called a range. The birds also may change their living routine with the seasons, which may be necessary for the birds' survival. Their summer range and winter range can be quite different. When fall comes and days become shorter, quail form larger coveys, roost in groups, and settle in an area where food will be more available throughout the winter.

If the habitat changes very little from year to year, the same range will be occupied by a family of quail. These areas are occupied on a regular basis because they have ideal food and cover arrangements that are attractive to the birds. The birds are not necessarily the carryover birds of the previous year, however. The turnover of a bobwhite population is high, but of the few birds that do survive through the winter, it not uncommon for them to occupy the same range the following year. Birds shifting or moving out of a range is a good indication of a lack of food or cover in that location.

The size of a range is important to the quail hunter looking for a covey, although it is not the only factor. The shape of the cruising radius also has to be considered. The size and the shape of a range can vary a great deal. We think of one covey per range, but if the habitat is abundant with food and cover, more than one covey may use the same area and overlapping is common. Not all areas are occupied by quail, even if they look good to us. Why some areas are used and others are not is not known. It could be birds need a certain amount of space or the habitat can carry only so many of that species. The food supply in relation to cover

Bobwhites are mostly ground dwellers and eat a wide variety of foods.

and its arrangement has to also be an important factor in site selection.

Within a range, birds have a home base, a place much like our living room. They use this home base daily, at different times of the day, depending on the weather. While weather does change the birds' daily routine, seasonal weather has the greatest affect on range movement.

FOOD AND WATER

Since the bobwhite is found over a wide range of the country, it is not surprising that its foods vary from one place to another. Singling out a bobwhite's favorite foods is impossible. On a southern plantation, lespedeza and smartweed seeds may be the birds' choice food, but in the Flint Hills of Kansas their favorite may be quite different. However, a large share of its food everywhere is found in farms fields; thus the bobwhite is generally associated with the tillage of the land. Certain woodland types with good supplies of mast are the exception to this generality. No matter where one hunts bobwhite, it's important to learn the birds' feeding habits and the kind of food

available in that area.

Bobwhites are mostly ground dwellers and eat seeds, fruits, greens and insects, a wide variety of foods in hundreds of combinations. The diversity of food is why the bird has such as wide distribution. A good diet is vital for the quails' existence.

When you're hunting, it may appear that food is always abundant, but that is simply not true. Fall is the time of plenty and food is usually abundant during the early part of the hunting season, but this surplus will not last until spring. Food diminishes throughout the winter making new vegetation and insects critical in the spring. Food also has to be available year-round close to cover. A healthy population of quail cannot be expected if food is scarce some years. Wild grains and agricultural crops produced every year close to good cover are what sustain an abundance of quail.

Bobwhites do not need free water to drink, but collect sufficient moisture from their food. Quail do congregate around surface water and will drink, but essentially bobwhites receive most of their water from seeds, insects and succulent greens.

DAILY ROUTINE

Around sunrise bobwhite begin to feed, primarily at edges and in open forests. A covey may start on foot toward a weed patch, crop field or other food area where the birds eat for an hour or two. Throughout their feeding period, the birds may collect grit, which aids in digestion, but is not essential. After several hours the birds will retire to a sheltered place for their midday rest. Throughout the day, the birds are not very active and spend much of their time resting, loafing and dusting. Coveys do move from place to place, however. Under normal circumstances daily movements are short. Even though bobwhite are mostly ground dwellers, many times a covey will get up and fly to a new location for reasons that remain a mystery. If disturbed, a covey will run or fly, taking the best escape route. During the day most activities occur under or near some type of cover. Rarely will a single bird be far from cover. Bobwhites return again to feeding places about two hours before going to roost.

Bobwhites prefer to roost in relatively open cover without canopy. The birds form a tight circle, with their tails pointing in and their heads out, ever alert for danger. Another advantage of being in a circle is their bodies are pressed together for warmth during cold nights.

HUNTING BOBWHITE

I'm walking past several rigid Brittanys on point, then a sudden explosion of whirling wings, the report of my gun, a retrieve and I'm holding a handful of feathers. This is the thrill I remember long after the hunting season is over.

My grandfather hunted bobwhites. I broke brush and did the bird dogging as a young boy. It was hard work, but I loved every minute of it. Later when I carried my first shotgun I hunted quail with a flushing dog, and he broke brush. Having a flushing dog helped, but to me a pointing dog seemed better.

Quail (all species) habitat and habits make them the ideal game bird for a pointing dog. But regardless of what kind of dog you have, you have to have a place to hunt.

Hunting preserves (paid hunting to shoot released gamebirds), quail plantations, or a local hunting guide take the worry out of finding a place to hunt. Finding the birds is the host's responsibility. Paying a fee for hunting wild birds also takes the worry out of finding a place to hunt and in many areas the price is reasonable. Leasing land to hunt quail is also growing in popularity, but bird populations can change from year to year.

The distribution of bobwhite quail is vast, but about 70 percent of the birds' land is privately owned. The rest is public. There are lots of public hunting lands available. Many state governmental agencies have leasing programs, wildlife management areas, and walk-in area programs available to bobwhite hunters. Federal agencies such as the U.S. Fish and Wildlife Service, the U.S. Army Corps of Engineers, the U.S. Bureau of Reclamation, the U.S. Bureau of Land Management and the U.S. Forest Service have public hunting available.

Today it is still possible to hunt private lands by getting permission from the land owner. In many areas it is not as hard as one thinks. I knock on a lot of doors and find it takes time, but is rewarding. No matter where you hunt it's helpful and satisfying to know the birds' habits and habitat.

A good pointing dog is essential for finding quail, but it's the hunter's responsibility to put the dog in bird country. You may have the best pointing bird dog in the country, but if you can't read the birds' habitat you are going to have limited success.

Knowing bobwhite cover and locating hunting territory go together. Without good cover, the territory will not be productive. To me, recognizing good bobwhite quail country is like a song in the play *The Music Man* — "You Gotta Know the Territory."

Scouting new territory prior to opening day can assure good hunting and save time once the season starts, but not all hunters have this opportunity. Scouting is important but not essential for a successful hunt. I hunt many different states, so scouting prior to opening season is out of the question. Far from home, I rely on hunting friends, the local Chamber of Commerce, and state and federal agencies to inform me of the hunting conditions and possible lands to hunt. If you are planning a trip to another state call ahead of the hunting season for information.

There are no hard and fast rules about hunting bobwhite quail. What works for me may not work for you. Each hunter should establish his or her own hunting method. For various reasons, most folks prefer not hunting alone.

The ideal combination for hunting bobwhites is probably two hunters with two dogs. A lot of bobwhite hunting is in high cover, over one's head. Two people can

A good dog is essential for finding bobwhite quail,
but it's the hunter's responsibility to put the dog in bird country.

hunt each side of a cover, and if there's a flush of quail, one person will have shooting. You have a better chance of marking a covey down after the flush with two people as well.

I'm not sure which is best, each hunter having their own dog or one hunter having a dog or two. Let me explain. If each person hunts their own pointer, that person knows the dog's capabilities, how it works birds, providing an advantage finding game. By each having their dog in the field, they can also separate and cover more ground. That's as long as the dog hunts for you and does not follow your partner's dog.

Years ago I hunted, as a rule, with only one partner. He didn't have a bird dog, nor did he have knowledge of the birds or the country. Needless to say, each time my dogs pointed I had a good idea of the birds' location and the direction the quail would flush because my dogs and I communicate.

There are disadvantages to each hunter having a dog in the field at the same time, however. Not all dogs get along. Others compete to flush a covey of quail. Still others won't honor and steal the point. Some play or antagonize one another while hunting.

Another disadvantage is two different people are calling out commands. I communicate vocally very little when my dogs are hunting. It confuses my dogs to have someone always blowing a whistle or yelling in the field. I have found, over the years, there are times my dogs' performance drops when a guest puts a dog down with mine. All of my dogs perform much better with their kennel mates. In fact, I have dogs that perform better in certain combinations. Some dogs like to hunt alone, others in pairs or with partners of their own sex. The point is, learn what's best for your hunting dogs and they will perform better for you.

Three people in a hunting party is okay as long as each knows the others' capabilities. The problem with three hunters is that usually one person is never in a good position to shoot. I do not recommend four people hunting together. If there are four in a hunting party, I suggest they split up into two groups as long as each party has a dog.

I like to hunt alone. Being alone with my dogs is special. By myself I can put down as many dogs as I like, and if one makes a mistake I don't have to explain it to anyone.

Lila Critz waits for a covey of bobwhite to clear the heavy cover before shooting.

I also enjoy hunting alone because every hunter who has a dog has a different philosophy of what a dog should do in the field. Here's my drill: a good dog hunts for his master, not for himself. As long as the dog is obedient, comes when called, backs other dogs and holds a point, he or she is free to run. I feel the actual hunting should be left to the dog. If the dog has a tendency to range far, I let him go. If the dog has a tendency to range close, that's okay too. I do not use hand signals, yell or wave direction, and I rarely use a whistle. But when I do it's to inform the dogs of my whereabouts or let them know I'm changing direction. I believe the best communication with a dog is silence. And caution should be taken about having too much control. Pointing dogs learn long before we do where the birds are. Let the dog hunt and just be a dog!

I also prefer to shoot alone. If I make a good shot or happen to get a double, it's satisfying, but I don't need to share experiences with someone else. For some reason, my shooting percentage goes down when I hunt alone. Maybe it's having no competitive pressures, or maybe it's because I don't have to make up excuses when I miss.

Most hunters, particularly young ones, hunt bobwhite cover too fast. I once did the same. Much of the time, bobwhite quail hunting is in hot weather and scenting conditions for a dog are poor. Good bobwhite cover is also dense and a dog can pass up bird scent easily. This is especially true if you are only running one dog. I use three or four pointing dogs and still miss birds when hunting heavy cover. I've hunted days when scenting conditions were so bad, that my dogs couldn't find a dead bird when they were standing on it. Many times I go over the same area within an hour and the whole hunting scene changes. Maybe its because a slight breeze has filtered through the cover or more moisture sifts into the air. I have found it works.

Weather Plays a Part: Many hunters follow the birds' daily feeding routine, hunting a couple of hours morning and evening. This is probably the easiest time for the dogs to find bobwhite quail because the birds are on the move and laying down a trail of scent. The weather also has a lot to do with when birds feed. On overcast days or when the weather changes, birds start feeding later in the morning and may feed most of the day. During severe weather, quail may fly to a feed patch, feed quickly and fly back to protective cover and spend most of the day there.

Most states have long bobwhite quail seasons. During a season the weather varies — hot, cold, dry, wet. Quail sense a weather change and respond accordingly. Even though a bobwhite is a creature of habit, every day in a quail's life is different, so every quail hunting day is different. I've had some of my best days when dark stormy clouds cover the western skies and I was hunting on the heels of a front.

Knowing the birds' habitats and daily routine, recognizing fresh bobwhite sign, knowing what to expect under various weather conditions, and a good pointer in top-notch physical condition are what makes great quail hunting. Be there when you can!

BOBWHITE HUNTING MYTHS

Hunting traditions are handed down through generations — parents to children, master hunter to novice hunter, landowner to landowner, landowner to hunter or outdoor writer to outdoor writer. All are guilty of fallacies because tradition often takes priority over knowledge or reason.

"When my grandfather farmed this place, dad said there were all kinds of bobwhite. As a boy he could shoot hawks and owls, and trapping predators brought in good money. You can't do that anymore. That's why the quail are gone," said the third-generation farmer, sitting on his green air-conditioned eight-wheel-drive tractor pulling a 60-foot chisel plow. Dust rose in the large, open, plowed field long after he stopped to talk to me.

In the past, predator control had its fling, with much promise and little logic, to protect and increase game bird populations in their natural environment. (Areas managed exclusively for wild or released bobwhites may be an exception.) But most studies show predation has little, if any, influence on wild game populations. In fact, predation may actually be beneficial in improving the gene pool and certainly plays a role in quail re-nesting attempts, expanding brood rearing over a longer period of weather conditions and insect production.

Another myth is that without surface water you won't have bobwhite quail. In a small town in Oklahoma, a young storekeeper told me of a great place to hunt bobwhites. He explained, "Not many folks know of its whereabouts. I was looking for grasshoppers to fish with and the birds scared the heck out me when they flew. The quail must have been getting a drink."

A little while later, I was driving along the main gravel road. On both sides were huge grain fields, cut lower than a gopher's belly. I turned off and went through a wide-open gate. Black dust rolled past the pickup as I followed the two-rut lane over the hill. The reservoir came into sight and disappeared again, folding within the huge cut grain field. Fifty or so ducks scooted off the large sky-blue pond and circled several times before I stopped the pickup.

The dogs found two coveys right where the young man saw them while he was bass fishing. The quail hang out around the reservoir for good reason, not because they need surface water but because it's the only place with good cover within a half mile.

In Louisiana, it seems more land is below sea level than above. Louisiana has a lot of small rural towns wrapped in swamps and at one time had an abundance of quail. A hunting friend from Shreveport who hunts swamp ducks told me, "Local duck hunters and turkey hunters look down at quail hunters because of the stories told about swamp quail being bigger and darker in color than other quail."

My friend continued, "Duck and turkey hunters spend a lot of time in the swamp and swamp quail are no different than any other quail. Quail hunters just try to make you think there is more meat in the pot."

Now as for the species "swamp quail," there is no such bird. But in the South the stories have been told so many times, most folks believe them. Cajun duck hunting stories have always been in question, as have tales about old mossy headed swamp turkeys that step on their beards while feeding and move up and down the bayous like migrating ducks. I suspect the same is true with swamp quail stories.

The myth of the swamp quail can be simply explained by the fact that all species have size and color variations. Many times a hunter kills an adult male quail, compares it with smaller juvenile birds and concludes it is a different species. I have witnessed different color characteristics in other upland game birds, many within a single covey or flock.

Another false belief has to do with the interbreeding of pen-raised quail with wild birds and the introduction of a foreign subspecies of bobwhites (Mexican quail) to our native species. The plaintiffs profess that the descendants have changed native quail behavior. They complain bobwhite quail coveys run instead of fly, flush wild and go much farther distances. And when a covey is flushed, it always heads for heavy cover and upon landing, runs or flies again.

Barbot Mc Millan, a true country gentleman, who knows bird dogs and bobwhites, has positioned Dale Critz for a good crossing shot.

It is habitat changes, however, that have affected Bobwhite behavior, rather than foreign genes getting mixed into the species. The ability of quail to adapt to external pressures does not happen overnight, but is a long process. The bobwhite that runs and flushes wild will live another day and pass that trait on to its offspring. In the 50 years I've hunted quail, I believe the bird has not changed, but its habitat has, which makes the quail react differently. Bobwhite quail run in open understory. Bobwhites have always run, and when hunted, can run as much as Western quail in sparse habitat. In fact, bobwhites run more than some Western quail species.

RUNNING BOBWHITES

A few years ago, I hunted for several days on my own in southern Iowa. Bobwhites were numerous and the population surpassed most years. Cold turkey, I stopped at a farmhouse, hoping to hunt bobwhites.

It was 10 o'clock, Saturday morning. An elderly man wearing bib overalls walked out of the pump house. I introduced myself:

"Sir; I'm Ben Williams from Montana. Would it be okay ...?"

He interrupted, "I see you're from Montana by your pickup plates and you want to hunt quail."

"Yes sir! Sure would," I said.

"Where are you from in Montana?" he asked.

"Livingston."

"Where is that from Bozeman?" he asked.

"Oh about 20 miles east of there."

"I have a son going to college there. It's nice country where you live," he said.

We walked to the house, had a cup of coffee and talked about the weather, farming, Montana, Yellowstone National Park and fishing. Back home when I talk to a rancher, I call it kicking gravel. We kicked a little gravel and he told me where to find the bobwhites.

Soon, I was hunting. No snow had accumulated, but nights were cold. By midday the sun hadn't shown, a light wind rattled the colorful leaves piled under the tall oak trees. It felt like winter was around the corner.

Mast lay everywhere under the oaks. Scratchings were abundant, signs of quail feeding on the edge of the forests. That day was cool, with a soft wind. The dogs seemed to float over the cover, kicking up big, bent, bright leaves at high speed, making sounds like squirrels running through

the forest. The dogs loved it. Running under the canopy of tall oaks, the mulch of dried leaves and the soft humus must have felt good underfoot.

A covey flushed wild. Shoe and Daisy ran downwind and slid to a rigid point, leaves floating past them as they stopped. The two twisted their bodies like corkscrews, windward, looking toward me, then fixing their eyes on the ground. I walked toward the brace of dogs and neither moved. I walked past them, then turned around. They still did not move. "Birds are gone," I said. "Lets go." No sooner were the words out of my mouth than a big bunch of quail got up in back of me. I spun around, too late for a shot. The two coveys split, one going right and the other straight ahead. I thought how many times I had done this. Both coveys must have been running. The dogs pointed again, this time downwind, just below where the two coveys took flight.

I marked one covey down, watching three birds pitch into a small brush pile, and I had a good idea where the other covey landed. I called both dogs in and walked a wide circle around where the three birds landed so the Brittanys could approach the birds downwind.

Both dogs slammed into a rock-hard point 6 feet from the brush pile. I was thinking double. The dogs rolled their eyes, but never moved as I walked in and kicked the brush. Both dogs broke, diving into the heavy cover. Two birds flushed from the far side of the brush pile, out of gun range. I never found the third bird that landed, nor the rest of the covey. I expanded the circle walking around where I thought the bird had landed. One dog made a halfhearted point and I killed a single flushing wild at about 15 yards. The young dog caught the wounded bobwhite airborne and retrieved the bird to hand. The rest of the day wasn't much different. Everything seemed to go wrong. The quail just wouldn't hold for the dogs.

Every quail hunting day is different. The next day I was hunting the same two coveys, just to see if the quail acted the same. The dogs were great, the bobwhites held like they were tied down, and shooting was easy. But there are more pleasures in quail hunting than the shooting.

Maybe it's just the good hunts we remember, when the dog does everything right, the quail fly up our pant legs and two birds fall after every rise. I haven't been in that situation very often, though.

BOBWHITES, OLD AND NEW

There are more ways to hunt bobwhites in North America than there are breeds of hunting dogs to hunt them. There are more philosophies of how pointing dogs should hunt bobwhites than there are vehicles designed to carry them. There are also more opinions about the kinds of guns and gauges one should use for shooting bobwhites than there are states in which the birds live.

But in the South, that is the Deep South, plantation quail hunting has a long history. It's as traditional as Southern fried chicken, black-eyed peas, and grits. This form of bobwhite hunting is steeped in tradition and its history rivals that of ruffed grouse in North America.

To the Southern gentry, bobwhite quail hunting is riding mule-drawn wagons, dog handlers on saddled horses, double guns (side-by-sides), English pointers, a Labrador retriever next to the wagon driver, and a plantation hunting course. To these folks, wild Southern bobwhite quail are the best of all birds for good dog work. English pointers are so consistently a part of bobwhite hunting that it's hard to imagine hunting a plantation without them. This form of hunting is still widespread on many Southern quail plantations.

With the growing popularity of sporting clays, these same folks are extending their shooting skills to hunt upland game birds. Quail hunting in the Deep South is growing by leaps and bounds. In fact, the growth in popularity of hunting all species of quail and other game birds in North America is phenomenal. And when there is growth, you have change.

For good reasons, some Southern plantation hunting traditions have changed, but certainly not their Southern hospitality. Today the Southern quail dog is followed on horseback or in some kind of rubber-tire vehicle. It may be mule-drawn, gas-powered, or an electric cart. Other than the mule-drawn wagon, these vehicles are not in the true tradition, but the results are the same — saving human foot power.

Today you can ride a horse, ATV four-wheeler, a golf cart, sit on a mule-drawn carriage or walk. Many hunters do walk. In fact, with the recent exercise craze, walk-up hunting behind pointing dogs is gaining ground in the South. I've been fortunate enough to have hunted behind plantation pointing dogs and their handlers in about every conceivable rig available. I have also followed plantation dogs on foot, which to me is still the most enjoyable.

Other breeds of pointing dogs have crept into the Southern plantation hunting scene because of these nontraditional methods of transportation. More people also have their own dogs. No matter what breed of pointing dog, every person that hunts with their own dog knows shooting is only one part of hunting quail. What comes before — the point, the covey rise, bringing up the gun — is as important as the shooting. Bobwhites bring the best out in a pointer, giving a dog the chance to strut its stuff, and the owner the opportunity to study his dog at work.

I've been hunting Dixieland quail for about a dozen years. Today, quail hunting in the South is pretty much restricted to private invitation or paying a fee. Many plantations are now commercial operations that accommodate the gowing number of hunters. Some have only wild birds, others have liberated birds, and others have both. I've done all three and have enjoyed every minute of it. Paid shooting can be arranged by the day or you can stay at a plantation for the whole traditional hunting experience. In many places you can also bring your own dog.

What about liberated quail? There are two methods of releasing birds. One is releasing a number of birds prior to the hunt. This "put and take" is efficient and economical. The other method, which is growing in popularity, is to release birds in groups prior to the hunting season so they can form coveys. By doing this the birds have a longer survival period in the wild. They can socialize the same as wild quail coveys, which is much more conducive to survival. Coveys also attract stray birds and other small coveys that have previously been shot at but missed. The early release program produces strong flying birds, much the same as their wild cousins.

No matter what type of Southern quail hunting you do, there is that feeling that you are a part of a great American tradition. Hunting a few days in January or February with the warm sun on your back, hearing the rustling and smelling the fragrant piney woods is long remembered.

A TRADITIONAL BOBWHITE HUNT

My everyday hunting apparel consists of a pair of strong legs, lug-soled moccasin-type boots, well-worn hunting pants, a beat-up vest and a baseball cap. This suits me fine, no matter what kind bird hunting I do.

BOBWHITE QUAIL

Although walking is my preference, I'll have to admit I have used other means of transportation while hunting Southern bobwhites. I found riding a mule-drawn wagon rewarding and am delighted to have had the chance to hunt in the grand old Southern tradition. Many plantations pride themselves on using the carriage exclusively for transporting their guests.

Here is a taste of what to expect when hunting in the true Southern tradition: Our hunting rig consisted of an open carriage, called a hunting wagon, drawn by a matched pair of mules. There were two rows of red Naugahyde cushioned seats, with enough space to accommodate the driver and five guests. Behind the seats were built-in dog boxes with storage above. A black Labrador retriever sat next to the wagon driver.

Two English pointers were working back and forth in front of the dog handler. He and his assistant were riding Tennessee walking horses. The lead dogs slowed, then pointed. The other dog backed instantly, then both dogs moved on. The same routine continued, then the brace of dogs stopped side by side, tails high, motionless. The two horsemen stood straight-legged in their saddles watching the dogs. The dog handler raised his hat above his head, signaling to bring the mules into position. The mules moved alongside the two horsemen, then stopped. The assistant requested the next two shooters to dismount from the wagon. The dog handler dismounted from his horse and handed the reins to the assistant.

It was my turn to shoot. I lifted the 28-gauge side-by-side from the wagon gun rack, stepped down and paused for my hunting partner to do the same. I loaded the shotgun but did not close the breech. I walked past the mules; the dogs held so there was no rush. Both of us hunters moved alongside the dog handler. The three of us walked past the two rigid pointers, the dog handler whipping the brush in front. For a moment all was still, then a burst of wings and a flush of quail. The covey swung to the left. I held up and didn't shoot, but my hunting partner put a bird on the ground. The pointers never moved. The dog handler signaled and called the Lab. The Lab jumped out of the wagon, ran toward the dead bird, and retrieved the quail to the wagon driver. The dog handler whistled and the two pointers moved on. We followed the dogs and looked for the singles. Both dogs pointed again and my partner and I each killed a quail that the Lab retrieved again. The handler informed us that three birds were enough out of a covey, so we stopped and unloaded our guns. The wagon pulled up alongside and we climbed aboard. The driver looked back at me and smiled. The procession moved on, the dogs looking for a new covey. It was the next two shooters' turn.

*In the deep south, plantation quail hunting has a long history of using mule-drawn wagons,
pointers and dog handlers working on saddled horses.*

This went on for a couple hours in the morning and again in the afternoon. Between the two shoots we were driven back to the plantation. There was time for a cocktail, if we wished, before the midday meal, and a half hour's rest before the wagon rolled again.

Horses, Horses: Now about another method of transportation. My good friend Dale Critz said, "Ben, we're going to hunt the first three days on our plantation, Cheeha-Combabee, then a couple of days on two other plantations of friends of mine. The first two days we'll use horses. The wagon makes too much noise."

My answer, over the telephone was, "Dale, what about walking?"

He said, "Too much country and the food patches are far apart on the courses we are going to follow. We'll get better shooting with horses. Also I'm asking a different guest each day to hunt with us and the first two days both of them like to ride horses. The last day my other guest is allergic to horses, so we'll walk, but that will be a walking course."

Now I was wondering why I didn't think of that. "All right. Horses it is."

You would think I would jump at the opportunity to ride horseback since I live in the Wild West, but I hadn't ridden for years, and I still prefer to walk when I hunt. To me, horses are a headache I don't need in the field.

Cheeha-Combabee plantation has fine Tennessee walkers and most of them are fairly short legged, with the exception of mine. David, my horse of their choice, is three hands higher than any other horse on the plantation. But my hosts and the horse handler assure me David is the most gentle horse on the place. The handler also suggests I use the tailgate of the pickup to get into the saddle. Being from cattle country, pride gets in the way, and I get on David without the help of the tailgate, but I do use a small rise in the ground to get my foot in the stirrup.

High up on a horse, it's a pretty sight to see dogs working. It is also a long way from the ground. Horses can sense a person who has ridden and after several minutes, David and I got along fine. I'm sure David knew he's had much better riders on his back than me. In the South the horse is still the original leg saver and is still used extensively on many plantations. At Cheeha-Combabee I will have to admit the habitat and terrain lends itself to hunting off horseback.

High on a horse, in piney woods, it's easy to see a dog point.

Cheeha-Combabee has been managed as hunting property for generations and quail hunting has always been an integral part of the plantation. The plantation does have some wild birds, but not enough for outstanding hunting. The practice of releasing quail onto the property began more than 30 years ago and has continued to the present. Cheeha-Combahee's practice is directed primarily at a preseason release. The plantation manager is a wildlife biologist. Another wildlife biologist, a bobwhite specialist, is directly involved in the overall management plan. I must say, this operation is first class. The coveys fly about as fast and as far as their wild cousins.

There was no reason to quicken the pace. Lila Critz's two Brittanys, Gussie and Winnie, would hold, but we sped up anyway. Lila sat high on her horse and marked down a couple of quail after the flush. Dale and I had each shot a single on the covey rise. We followed the dogs beyond where Lila thought the bird had landed. Both dogs searched the area but found nothing. I flushed a single as we walked back to the horses, but didn't raise the 28-gauge because the bird cut in front of the oncoming horses. After flushing the single, the dogs combed the area and each pointed a bird.

Dale tumbled one. The other buzzed around a pine and then toward heavy cover. Then the horses flushed three more birds coming towards us.

I thought that we must have walked right by them the first time, not giving the dogs a chance to thoroughly work the cover. We got back on our horses and the dogs were sent on. The two Brittanys found three more coveys, the last about sunset. All in all, we didn't harm the quail population.

Three days of hunting liberated birds at Cheeha-Combabee convinced me that programs like these are outstanding and help sustain good hunting in the region. Preseason released birds are not much different than hunting wild birds. The pointers act the same, the shooting is fast and the charm of hunting Southern bobwhite is still with us. It may not be for everyone, but it is a wonderful opportunity for a true Southern experience.

BOBWHITE HUNTING IN THE MIDWEST

I've been going to the Midwest to hunt bobwhites for the past 20 years. The Midwest certainly has more accessible country to hunt wild quail. States such as Iowa, Missouri, Kansas, Texas and Oklahoma all have good wild populations of birds. When you hunt the Midwest, your choices are hunting private land (if you know someone), hunting public land, hiring a professional guide or visiting a hunting lodge, all of which can be over wild birds. Overall the Midwest has a lot more wild birds than Southeastern states, but the bobwhite hunting agenda for the Midwestern hunter is quite different than that of their Southern counterparts. The way of the Midwestern bobwhite hunter is walking behind a pair of big running pointing dogs, shooting wild birds, using automatics or pump shotguns, hunting the singles after the flush, thanking the farmer after the hunt and driving home late in your pickup.

My first hunting trip with Wendell Holeman was on my turf, the Rocky Mountain front. Our second trip was on his homeground, the Flint Hills of Kansas. The habitat of the bobwhite in the Midwest differs from that of their cousins in the East, but it is still the same fine bird. Quail hunting has also become a tradition in the Midwest, and in some years Kansas has the finest anywhere.

The Flint Hills have a peaceful presence, like the people who live there. In some areas, crop fields are small, bisected by gravel and dirt roads. The fence rows are wide and brushy with many edges. Old homesteads dot the landscape and their hedges and windbreaks of osage-orange, Russian olives, caragana and green ash are good places for quail to hide. Still other parts of the prairie grassland are much like they were before the settlers arrived. The grass seems to roll and tumble like ocean waves touching a brilliant cobalt sky, and the quail are here in great numbers as well. The two different habitats make up both of Wendell's hunting grounds.

I spent a couple of mid-December days in the Flint Hills hunting bobwhite with Wendell, his wonderful pointers and a friend. Wendell is a retired public school administrator who works full time at his passions of training bird dogs, hunting quail and judging field trials.

The week before I arrived, the Flint Hills got more than a foot of snow. Kansas does not often experience extended periods of deep snow, but the first day we hunted, snow still covered part of the ground, therefore getting to prime quail country was difficult.

We met our friend Dave and discussed things like mud, snow and where to go without getting stuck. We eventually set off and after several miles on a gravel road, turned into a CRP field and parked alongside an old fence. A wide stand of caragana covered the strands of barbed wire. The understory below the canopy of the shrubs was open. A covey of quail watched our arrival from its safety, then scurried down the fence line and out of sight.

On the left side of the fence, the large CRP field was full of tall weed stalks, their empty seed pods glistening in the sun. Below the high weeds, the golden brown grass was bent almost flat from the recent snow. Small patches of snow dotted the meadow. To the right was a muddy harvested cornfield. At the far end of the meadow was a grass slough too wet to plow and surrounded by sumac, its dried fruit still hanging. Across the shallow slough was a woodlot and then another cornfield.

The location was perfect for quail. As Wendell pointed out the aforementioned birds, Dave walked over to our pickup and the two discussed which dogs to put down. No one was in a hurry. We had all morning to hunt.

They put two dogs down — Dave's dog, Jack and Wendell's, Jock — both of which pointed the minute they hit the ground. After several points along the fence, a single quail flushed a hundred yards ahead and flew toward the grassy slough at the end of the field.

We worked both fields on each side of the fence, but never did find the covey. I assumed the birds had flown in the same direction as the single without us seeing them, but Wendell and Dave weren't so sure. The two dogs made several more casts in the dense, overgrown field but with no success. We looked for the single, thinking we might find the covey in the woods, and the birds flew toward a long brushy draw. Both dogs found several singles, and both guns collected a bird or two.

We put up two more coveys that morning, had great dog work, shot a few more quail and then headed back for lunch. Wendell suggested we look once again for the lost covey, so on the way back we took the route — the weedy CRP field — toward the pickup. A slight breeze was moving the high weeds. Jock and Jack were running hard out in front of us, their heads high, when they locked up like stones.

There was no doubt in my mind the dogs had found the covey. It seemed to be in about the same spot the dogs first pointed, in the overgrown weedy field. Why they did not find the covey at first is not clear to me. Maybe it had something to do with the snow or the bent grass not releasing bird scent. I will never know, but maybe one reason I have such a passion for bird hunting is that every day is so different. After the flush and the blur of wings, the sound of two crisp shots echoed from the wood and feathers drifted down following the gentle breeze, settling on the tall weed pods.

Wendell Holeman is a dog expert—you can see it in his pointers' eyes.

Getting a double on bobwhites is difficult, but good quail hunting is still available in North America.

GONE WITH THE QUAIL

I'm was talking to a young man, while we followed his flushing dog across the Montana prairies. Still living at home in a small town in South Carolina, he looked elsewhere to hunt after the quail population plummeted in his home state. He told me bobwhite quail were once numerous, and he and his father spent hours hunting together. He said that across America, good bobwhite hunting is gone and the gray partridge has become its replacement.

I disagree. Huns are covey birds and act much like bobwhite, but in many areas of the bobwhites' range hunting is still supreme and Western quail species have the same hunting attributes as bobwhites. My point is this — even though many places east of the Mississippi no longer have quality quail hunting, there is still plenty of good quail hunting available in North America. One only has to look to find it.

Chapter Two
VALLEY QUAIL

*I can trace my first covey of valley quail to the Northwest, beyond the Rocky Mountains
in the Okanogan Valley. Since then, I have changed my thinking about them.*

Washington: It was mid-October and I was driving along the Columbia River following Route 97. My destination was the Okanogan Valley. The water was low, too deep blue to be translucent. Steep canyon streams pour tons of glacial mountain water into the Columbia River each spring and summer. Now, the canyon highway bridges seemed too high and wide. The pools far below were not connected and the boulders were the size of my blue Volkswagen.

Chelan, Okanogan, Omak, then Riverside showed on the land, and I pulled over near the Okanogon River. My two Brittanys, Gina and Lola, bailed out of the blue Bug and drank, paw deep in a clear feeder stream that ran into the main stem. I decided to fill my canteen and walked up the creek looking for a deep pool. The leafless trees allowed me

to see a long way up the tumbling stream. I squatted down to fill the canteen. The dogs arrived, kicking sand in the pool. Several pools ahead, a water ouzel (dipper) popped up from underwater, rode downstream a short distance and flew low overhead scolding us for being present.

I headed north, drove for an hour and 20 minutes, then turned off the main highway onto a gravel road, dust blowing past me faster than I could go. The road came to a dead end. I stopped, opened a wire gate, turned right onto a dirt lane, stopped again, closed the gate, and continued driving over several hills. Soon I was parked next to a small spring by an abandoned farmstead. The old buildings lay in a narrow valley with steep hills and draws on both sides. One end of the valley seemed boxed in. The creek turned and the hills appeared to merge together.

Jim Bier knows where the valley quail hide.

I set up camp inside the old barn, hoping it would rain, but I believed that was wishful thinking. It hadn't rained in a month. I got the tent up, sleeping bag and duffel bag in place. I was ready to set up the kitchen. The two dogs were running around the junk piles looking for rabbits. I crafted a makeshift table, then a bench that I put next to the spring. I collected some wood for a fire.

Gina and Lola came back. They must have heard me getting food out of the grub box. I built a fire, opened a can of chili and a can of dog food. I burrowed a hole in the coals, placed the can of chili in the fire and waited. Later, we ate.

It was about dark when I put the grub box in the Volkswagen. As I walked back, a great horned owl glided out of a large cottonwood tree and landed on top of an old wooden tower. There was no evidence of the windmill's blades anywhere. The owl twisted its head from side to side looking down. I stopped under the derrick, looked up and the owl flew off.

The dogs and I crawled into the tent. I lay awake thinking about what the rancher said. "When I cut the hay meadow, chukars came from the hills to eat grasshoppers. Chukars were around the water while I worked on the stock dam in the big draw — the draw that leads down to the homestead There's also a spring above the dam. Water comes out of a hillside and I heard birds calling up there." Then, later, having thought about the situation, he said, "Sometimes I see them in the bottoms of the draws while I'm driving. Try along the main creek. I've seen them there too, along with those other little birds that run like crazy when you drive toward them—quail, I think."

I was still thinking. I was after chukars and they were all over the place. No cattle had been on the premises for a long time. Even though the meadows were cut, there seemed to be too much brushy cover along the creek for chukars. The meandering creek didn't fit my idea of chukar habitat. The bottoms of the draws and side hills were the best bet. I'd start hunting the main draw, working my way to the stock tank.

A coyote yipped, then yip-yipped again. The two dogs moved closer to the sleeping bag. It sounded like a ridgeline coyote, maybe two, traveling together yipping, singing like flutes in the night.

Next morning I tried to get a fire started. The wood was damp. The mute-colored short grass spread over the hills like a silent wave, yet to be awakened by the morning sun or light breeze. The hills were too high for an early morning sunrise or solar wind. The tall, overgrown grass inside the gray, dilapidated picket fence that surrounded the large frame house was covered with splashes of light frost.

While we waited for the fire to catch and the coffee to boil, the dogs and I walked around the old, but once stately, white picket fence. The abandoned house, the best-preserved building there, had weathered wood and rusty nails. It was a two-story wood-and-brick home, once chalk white. The porch was held up by fluted columns. A high gamble roof with four dormers seemed to touch blue sky. Protruding from the mossy slate roof were three brick chimneys. A row of large cottonwoods led to a carriage building and long bunkhouse. Beyond that was the big barn I was staying in and several small outbuildings whose use I couldn't identify. Why would anyone let a house like this go to ruins? Maybe it was too far from town, or someone's dreams gone astray.

The sky was cloudless. The sun was peeking over the hill, but the homestead was still in shadow. That morning I felt winter coming. The hot coffee and sweet roll tasted good. The two Brittanys were growing impatient, so I hurried. I decided not to carry a lunch, but to come back and cook something hot.

Over my shoulder I carried a Browning A5 automatic 12-gauge shotgun with a poly-choke (an adjustable choke attached to the end of the barrel). It was heavy. I purchased it a couple of years before for hunting pheasants. After seeing these hills, a lighter shotgun would have been better. I said to myself, "Why didn't I bring my Lefever double-barrel 16-gauge shotgun? It's much lighter."

It was easy at times like that to wonder if I'd made the right choice. Maybe the birds would be along the meadow feeding early in the morning instead. But the grasshoppers were almost all gone.

My plan was still the same as the previous night. I walked past the old outbuildings, then a caved-in root cellar. I stopped and looked for old bottles, picked up a couple of tin cans and tried to figure out what their contents had been. Beans, I thought. I started up the sloping terrace toward the stock dam. The west half was in sunlight, so I moved to that side. The dogs hadn't started to stretch out, so I encouraged them. Gina and Lola moved out a bit farther. There was no sign of any birds.

After 15 minutes, I estimated the stock dam was getting close. Soon, I was hoofing it up a steep grade. I stopped to catch my breath and I heard a chukar call. I listened. *Chuck, chuck, chuck chuck*. That was followed by *per-chuck-per-chuck-per-chuck* and then with increased intensity and volume the call becme three syllables, *chuck-a-ra, chuck-a-ra, chuck-a-ra*. I climbed to the top of the grade and looked into the stock dam. The reservoir was surrounded by a small basin. At least 25 chukar flushed and flew up the side hill in the direction of the chukar single calling. Watching the birds fly, I saw a bird standing on a rocky vantage point. I assumed it was the bird that was calling.

Then more started calling. Even others on the opposite side of the dam answered. The whole basin came alive with sounds. *Chuck, chuck, chuck, Chuck-a-ra, chuck-a-ra, chuck-a-ra*. This got our attention. Up we went.

Five was the limit. The shooting was over within an hour, even though I missed a few chukars shrieking down the hillside. The dogs did their job and then rested while I cleaned the birds by the reservoir. I've heard tales of chukar hunting, but this time I got them flat-footed. I was back at camp before noon. I hung the five birds inside the cool barn. The weather had warmed up. Instead of having a hot meal I ate a bologna sandwich and drank an orange soda. Both Gina and Lola were curled up under the makeshift table next to my legs. Valley quail popped into my mind. I had my limit of chukars, but the rancher did say something about quail along the creek.

Washington state hunting regulations were tucked in the Volkswagen's glove box. I had a look. California quail (Valley quail) Oct. 12 - Jan. 12, Daily Bag Limit 10, Possession Limit 30. For a moment, I wished I had my Lefever double-barrel 16-gauge shotgun. But I didn't and I had no idea what to expect hunting these quail anyway.

For the first half-hour there was no sign of quail. I walked in the cut meadow, following the creek. I encouraged the two dogs to hunt the heavy cover, but like me they were more interested in walking the open meadow. It was easier.

After walking over a mile and crisscrossing the dry creek, I gave up on the flat ground and looked toward the hills. One draw looked as good as the next, so I called the dogs in and took the next draw I saw.

I was surprised to see a trickle of water coming down the draw. The source was someplace above. I walked farther and went around a sharp bend. The draw narrowed, then opened. To my amazement, the sides were no longer steep.

Both hillsides were wind-bleached grass, tall common sagebrush and low junipers. Patches of cheatgrass were strung along the old cattle trails — trails that led to a spongy seep. The bottom of the draw was full of tall buffaloberry bushes, scrub chokecherries and other mixed hardwoods. Wild blackberry vines climbed, finger-like, following deep crevices up the hills on both sides of the draw. Beyond here there had to be a larger water source. In summer this must be a wildlife oasis.

Well ahead of me, the two dogs got to the first stand of tall buffaloberry bushes. Then came a sound, *oh-HI-oh, oh-HI-oh, oh-HI-oh.* A bunch of valley quail flushed, flying up the side of the hill and landing in sagebrush. Others flew and landed in a long string of blackberry briars. Still others ran through the open understory of the buffaloberry bushes, toward the chokecherries.

I called the dogs back and hurried my pace. The runners flushed in a wave and scattered among the group that landed in the sage. Five or six more flushed from the other side of the buffaloberry bushes, out of shotgun range as I walked by. Gina pointed ahead of me, moving toward where the quail on the ground flushed. I kept walking, following the dog as she pointed and broke, pointed and broke.

Then she stopped and pointed, rock solid. There were more quail running on the ground, and I knew I must keep up with the dogs. A single flushed. I shot, missed, reloaded. Three more birds flushed and I shot twice more, but nothing fell. Two more quail got up while I was reloading.

I was disgusted — I shot three times and not a single feather. I called the dogs back and looked up the hillside where most of the birds had gone. I figured there were more than 100 valley quail scattered in the draw.

I wished I had my Lefever. The Browning automatic 12-gauge never seemed to fit me and I wasn't sure the poly-choke worked. I twisted the choke and realigned the marks to "IM" (improved choke). We crossed the bottom of the draw and started up the slope. A third of the way up, I paused and listened to get a fix on a bird's position above me. Quail were calling everywhere. Gina pointed a large sagebush. I walked next to her, turned my head and saw Lola pointing another sage plant to my right. Both birds buzzed out like little rockets. I snap-shot and missed. This seemed to go on forever. Point, flush, miss. Point, flush, miss. I was getting more disgusted by the minute.

I was in the dumps as I worked downhill, following a line of blackberry briars. Both dogs pointed momentarily and a little dark blur screamed by. Without thinking, I swung fast, snapped off a shot, and finally a cloud of feathers. The quail plowed into a sagebush and feathers followed, drifting past the top of the sage. The dogs were nowhere in sight. I picked up the small cock, smoothed the bird's iridescent topknot and slipped it in my vest.

By day three, I had close to the possession of chukars, but not even a day's limit of California quail. I had burned up plenty of powder for a few small birds, but the effort was well worth it.

I daydreamed as I drove back. Chukar hunting is fun, but western quail hunting was my new goal. A light 20-gauge side-by-side or an over-under shotgun, improved cylinder and modified chokes, using 7½ or 8 shot, would be just the ticket for valley quail.

The Columbia River was dark like the sky that evening. The water was no longer blue like my Volkswagen. Shadows danced on the river's surface.

KNOWING THE BIRD

Valley Quail Origins: Valley quail or California quail? California quail have seven recognized subspecies that live in different and distinct types of habitat. All of these subspecies live in California or Baja, California. Even though all the races are a member of one species, there are some differences in each subspecies' appearance, but the difference is so slight that it usually takes a taxonomist to identify a particular subspecies.

The subspecies Valley California Quail (*L. c. californicus*) has the largest native range, and this subspecies is the foundation of the re-stocking programs throughout the Far West. There is also evidence of some mixing of the different races of quail involved in the transplant programs. Since this game bird has been so successfully distributed throughout the Northwest, both names are used today. John James Audubon called them valley quail (*Lophortyx californicus*) and that's the name I prefer, even though the name "California quail" may be preferred by taxonomists. Take your choice!

No matter which name you use, the bird is elegant, graceful and has a handsome plumage. It's a sportsman's bird, a fast flier, a deceiving target and one of the liveliest of all American game birds.

VALLEY QUAIL

A female quail sits in a tangle of brush; it's not unusual to find a whole covey of valley quail off the ground.

Long before the Spaniards set foot on the land we call California, the aboriginal indigenous people trapped and hunted valley quail. The natives used the birds for food and to decorate their ceremonial dress.

With the rapid settlement of California during and after the Gold Rush, thousands of quail fell to the gun. The hunting was done mostly by ordinary working men using shotguns. The abundance of California quail during this period, according to records, is phenomenal. In good quail country, you could expect to see 1,000 or more birds in a single draw or around a watering hole. Where the birds gathered in large numbers, a hunter could kill 20 or more birds in a single shot. Today, stories of hunters harvesting hundreds of birds in a single day are hard to believe.

During the days of the California land settlements, there were few jobs and gold fever had faded, so folks turned to other means of making a living. After the land grab, thousands of men turned to market hunting everything from big game to quail, and every edible creature in between. Many of these men were excellent woodsmen, like field biologists who studied and knew their prey better than most hunters today.

Then came the development of agriculture. Lands were cleared of brush and trees. Quail have a fondness for fruits and vegetables and they raided vineyards, orchards and vegetable fields. Farmers complained bitterly of the destruction by quail and welcomed market hunters. Market hunters turned to large-bore shotguns, traps and nets. Quail were killed by the thousands. Some market hunters killed upwards of 1,000 quail a week.

During the quail marketers' heyday, birds were an important commodity. Wild game birds were in great demand in the big city markets. It was commonplace to see hundreds of upland game birds and waterfowl hanging in the front of meat markets. Millions of game birds were delivered to these markets in the San Francisco Bay area alone. While the number of quail taken was tremendous, little evidence suggests it went to waste.

Many sportsmen throughout the United States became concerned about the decline of the numbers of game birds. By the late 1920s wildlife conservation in North America was an earnest enterprise. At the federal and state levels a sequence of programs were initiated. Conservation agencies and fish and game departments were created. The effect of these established programs is what restored valley quail to much of their original range. The market hunters had to find other ways of making a living, and the "good old days" of shot-gunning came to a close. Though present populations of quail are low in some areas of California, in other areas they exceed the historic numbers. With the outcry in recent years of the decline of quail in some areas of the birds' present range, much attention has been given to improving the birds' environment.

DISTRIBUTION

The valley quail is originally native only to California and a few counties of Oregon and Nevada bordering the Golden State. Valley quail have been successfully introduced to many areas in the Northwest. The extension of the valley quail range through transplants is noteworthy and covers a much larger area than the birds' historic range. This extension has been mostly north and east of the birds ancestral range, the area called the Great Basin.

Today the valley quail is the most common and widespread quail in the west. It is found in the interior agricultural valleys, desert edges and the lower elevations of Washington, Oregon, California, Idaho, Nevada and Utah. The valley quail is also found in lower British Columbia, Baja, California and the Mexican peninsula.

Most of my valley quail hunting has been in Oregon, Washington and Idaho. The state of Oregon is a good example of the expansion of the valley quail's range. The valley quail is a native of Oregon, but was originally found only in a few counties. Due to extensive transplantation programs, present-day populations cover all of the birds' suitable habitat in the state. Today the valley quail is Oregon's most widely distributed game bird. The major reason for this is that valley quail are extremely adaptable. The bird is established not only in agricultural lands, sagebrush country and along riparian areas, but in urban areas as well. Within its location, the birds' needs are rather specific, even though they eat a wide variety of food. Like all species of quail, valley quail need combinations of open and closed cover: brushy cover for escape routes, open feeding areas close to cover and adequate roosting cover above ground. It is in the hunter's interest to encourage federal and state agencies to promote more conservation programs to protect and improve quail habitat. It is also important for quail hunters to join and contribute to conservation organizations such as Quail Unlimited to support habitat projects that promote healthy populations of not only quail species, but other upland game and songbirds.

Approximate range of the valley quail.

IN THE BUSH, IN THE HAND

Remember the sound *oh-Hi-oh, oh-HI-oh, oh-HI-oh* on your last hunting trip? It's the call of the valley quail. If you haven't heard that sound, you should. It's the most commonly heard call during the hunting season. To put a call from a wild bird into words is next to impossible. To me, the valley quail's assembly call also has a high-pitched metallic ring to it, *oh-HI-oh*.

Like all North American quail, the valley quail is a beautiful, small game bird. The adult male is plump-bodied and a trifle larger than a bobwhite. He weighs about 7 ounces, is 11 inches long and has a wingspan of 12 inches. The valley quail has two black teardrop-shaped topknot feathers that curve over the forehead. The forehead is sooty white and there is a skullcap of brown with a white border. The male's throat is black with a white border. The upper breast is slate blue and the nape of the neck blue-gray, with small white dots. The valley quail's back, wings and tail are dark blue-gray. The sides of the body are brownish-gray with white streaks. The bill is black, the eyes brown and the feet and legs are brownish-black. The female is pale and overall grayer than the male. She does not have white facial marking and her topknot is much smaller.

A male valley quail scurries to heavy cover.

The range of their close relative the Gambel's quail, *Lophortyx gambelii*, overlaps the valley quail's range in several locations. The valley quail and the Gambel's quail are similar in coloration, size and general habits, though most of their habitat is different. These two species look so much alike they can be easily confused by the hunter in the field. But upon close examination, the male and female of both species have different distinctive markings on their lower breast and belly.

The lower breast-belly feathers of the Gambel's quail are yellowish and in the middle of the breast-belly area is a large black spot, whereas the valley quail's lower breast-belly has distinctive whitish scaly markings and in the middle of the belly there is a chestnut patch.

LIFE CYCLE AND BEHAVIOR

Winter coveys of valley quail usually break up in late January, depending on the time of pairing in that location. The latitude, altitude and local climate dictate the time of breeding and egg laying in an area. In southern California, peak periods of egg laying occur April to June. In northern Washington peak periods are May to July. Twelve to 14 eggs are the average clutch for valley quail. They normally bring off one brood a season. If the nest is lost to predators,

accidents or another cause, the hen will lay a second, or even a third clutch, but there will be fewer eggs. If this happens, young birds will be different in size in the same area. Therefore, seeing different sizes of chicks does not mean a single pair of birds produced two broods. Double brooding is unlikely in most of the birds' range. There is some evidence a pair of quail could bring off two broods in the southern range if weather conditions are favorable for reproduction, but ideal weather patterns are rare.

Most nest sites are on the ground, but unlike other quail, valley quail have been known to build nests in low bushes, haystacks and on other elevated objects. Valley quail are good at hiding their nests and selecting a site where the female can approach and leave without being seen. The nest itself is a shallow hollow lined with dry grass, well concealed with growing vegetation overhead.

Incubation takes 22 to 23 days and is done entirely by the female. The male stays in the vicinity of the nest during incubation and is continually alert and attentive to his mate. If the female is killed, the male may assume her duties. The male does have an important role in rearing the young.

Following hatch of the last chick, the adults attend the young, leading them away from the nest. Both parents use

Footprints in the sand are a telltale sign of quail present.

calls to communicate with the young, such as feed calls, alarm calls and assembly calls. These calls are important in keeping the young birds alive and together as a single unit. The adults search out safe openings so the young birds can learn to catch insects and find other food on the ground.

Brood losses can be substantial during the first several weeks of life. Wet and chilling weather has a great effect on the chicks and it also reduces the number of insects that the young birds depend on for protein early in life. Good habitat is also an important factor for chicks. It creates overhead cover and produces more insects.

For the first two weeks of a chick's life, it is unable to regulate its own body temperature and depends upon the hen for warmth. At night the hen protects the young from the cold under her fluffy body feathers. During the day, the sun warms the chicks by heating up the ground and drying out the foliage.

The quail's day does not begin as early as other birds. With the first signs of the new day on the horizon, songbirds become restless and move about in search of food. The hen quail and her family wait for the earth to warm up. Late morning the young birds feed for an hour or so, then the hen leads them into a shady area during the heat of the day. The chicks rest, dust, loft and chase insects throughout midday. In early afternoon, the adults moves the young birds to a feeding area. Before the sun gets low in the sky she calls the brood together, moves them to a safe roosting place and gathers her chicks under her for the night.

Where is the male during all this time? He is like a gladiator, always alert, and at the first sign of danger sounds a warning call, causing the chicks to scurry for cover. He will attack any intruding creature that threatens the brood. It may be a mouse, roadrunner, or snake. No matter the size, he stands his ground. Sometimes even the hen gets into the ruckus. Unlike many game birds, valley quail rarely use the broken wing maneuver to decoy an intruder.

Chicks' feather development is rapid and they can fly a short distance in about two weeks. Young birds, like the adults, will first run from an intruder and then flush. They do not follow their parents when flushed, but scatter in all directions to the closest heavy cover. As summer advances, young quail become more mobile and their cruising range increases. At eight weeks the young quail are half grown and can run almost as fast as the adults. They are also capable of flights like the parents. As winter approaches, juveniles go through two molting changes and are fully grown with adult plumage in 14 to 16 weeks.

HABITAT

Valley quail live in a wide assortment of covers and there are many variations of habitat within each of these types. How valley quail use the habitat is determined by the kind of vegetation available, the climate, and the seasonal weather. Whether the region is desert, foothills, grasslands, dry or irrigated crops, it has to have non-woody and woody cover vegetation. Standing water is not a necessity in most areas, with the exception of extremely arid desert conditions, which lack succulent greens and insects.

The distribution of food, cover and water are the important factors that influence covey movement. Each type of habitat also has to provide food, moisture, roosting, nesting and loafing or escape routes. Valley quail habitat comes in five general types: range grasslands, dry-land farming, irrigated cropland, desert lands and suburban sprawl. Populations vary in each of these five ecosystems because of the birds' needs.

Open rangelands can be the best or the worst for quail populations, depending on the amount of brushy cover. My choice, and the best hunting in open range, is land not over grazed and with uneven topography interspersed with trees, brushy draws, weedy areas and moderate rainfall. This is ideal and fits all the birds' requirements. Grasslands within mixed sagebrush and plains forest communities also can have outstanding valley quail hunting.

I enjoy hunting desert country. Desert and semi-arid shrub grassland usually provide food, good mixed brush and evergreen shrubs or trees. In years when water is available, desert habitat can support a large quail population. Valley quail seem to belong there, like their cousin the Gambel's quail. There is a loveliness about hunting valley quail in a wide-open desert setting. Maybe it's because it is so isolated.

Dry-land farming usually lacks cover but has plenty of food. If a dry-land farming area has rolling hills with patches of grassy, unplowed ground, brushy areas around water courses or tree-lined draws, it can be productive for quail. Some of these places are out of the way but have large concentrations of coveys in isolated areas.

Irrigated lands have plenty of water and can have good food. However, many farmers have changed their methods to overhead sprinklers and no longer use waterways and ditches, which provide outstanding quail hunting. Walking a weedy creek bottom with open, cut meadows on both sides brings back memories of many days of some of the finest valley quail hunting I've ever had.

I have hunted valley quail in four of the five general habitat types. In the suburban sprawl areas around ranches or farm buildings, there are certainly plenty of quail. There is no more delightful bird to have around a yard than a covey of valley quail, but in these areas they should be enjoyed by the bird watcher or backyard biologist, not the hunter.

To summarize habitat from a hunting strategy, this is the main rule: valley quail are birds of brushy cover. The bird's preferred habitat is weedy cover around grasslands and mixed farming such as fallow fields, hedgerows and hardwood thickets. The best kind of brushy cover within arid ranges is not overgrazed by cattle or denuded by clean farming practices. Areas crucial for valley quail are dense escape cover along waterways, gullies full of thick cover, unused corners of pastures, abundant homesteads and well-managed public lands of shrub brush prairie and savannas. Bushy cover to valley quail is as important as sagebrush is to sage grouse.

FOOD AND WATER

"They are seldom found far from water." That's what the landowner told me the first time I hunted his place. He was right, but that is not true in all of the valley quail's range. I have found valley quail several miles from water in the heat of the day; although, I may not have been aware of all the watering holes or seeps.

Generally speaking, valley quail drink very little and not every day. Like other upland game birds, if succulent greens and insects are available and the weather is not blistering hot, quail can survive without ground water. But if succulent greens and juicy insects are available there is usually some type of moisture around.

In an arid landscape quail need ground water because desert habitat does not provide adequate plant or insect moisture. Droughts in the desert are not unusual and daily temperatures can soar. Even though birds need open water in the desert, that does not mean they have to have water every day. So it is possible, even in arid country, that valley quail can be a long way from free-standing water. In the desert environment, or any other type of habitat, the water source has to have cover close by or quail will not use it. Open water for livestock many times does not have any cover close by and is of no use to quail.

Valley quails' food supply has to be available year-round because they do not move great distances. It must be remembered there are many areas where food is more than adequate, but only for part of the year. In most of the birds' range food is a key element to sustaining a high population, but all the other key environmental elements also have to be present.

Quail do have seasonal shifts. The home range of a covey of valley quail is quite limited, usually less than three-quarters of a circular mile, even though some banded birds have been known to travel over three miles. But these long distances are mostly single birds mixing with other coveys, as other game birds do. This trend is sometimes called the "fall shuffle."

There are two different kinds of food shortages: long-term and short-term. Short-term shortages are usually caused by weather, such as snow, rain or flooding. Valley quail are somewhat vulnerable to severe winter conditions. Even though there can be substantial losses during a short-term food shortage, they do not have a devastating effect on the future population of birds in an area.

Long-term food shortages do have a lasting effect. Overgrazing of rangelands, especially public lands, results in reducing the carrying capacity or eliminating the quail population altogether in that area. Moderate grassland grazing produces more green forbs and weed seeds and generally benefits quail. Intensive farming practices (clean farming), and weed-free vineyards and orchards completely eliminate food, cover and quail.

Valley quail are primarily ground feeders and seed eaters by choice. Annual weed seeds make up a large portion of the birds' food, but quail will feed on whatever is available throughout the year. In fall, all kinds of weed seeds, grain, greens, insects, fruits and mast are consumed. In winter, some dried fruit and grain are available, but birds are mostly dependent on greens. Legumes make up a large portion of the greens eaten. In the spring birds feed mostly on greens and insects. Summer is the time of plenty—greens, weed seeds, grains, fruit, mast and insects are all eaten.

The food of the young quail is practically the same as the adults.' During the first several weeks of a chick's life, insects amount to more than half of the young birds' diet. Insects provide protein that chicks need for rapid growth.

DAILY ROUTINE

Valley quail are gregarious and form large social groups in late fall that stay together until early spring. This social time period is also the quail hunting season. Even though we call them coveys, they are actually several coveys or family groups consisting of parents, their offspring and other non-family birds. These large coveys of sometimes 100 or more birds perform all daily activities as a group. The whole group also roosts together at night.

Unlike most other quail species, valley quail roost off the ground. Their preference is dense evergreens, but they also use low shrubs or trees. If water is available, birds will roost near it. They get up after sunrise, but if the weather is rainy or cold they fly down much later. Before any birds leave the roost, a male or two will call several times. This good morning call is, *oh-Hi-oh, oh-HI-oh.*

In late fall or winter, coveys band together near available food supplies. Quail feed principally in the morning and then again in the late afternoon. Each feeding period is about two hours, unless the weather is foul and then they feed much longer. Once morning feeding is over, the birds move to a convenient place that is sheltered by overhanging tangled cover.

During this time of the day, birds rest, feed off and on, dust in powdery soil, or hang around a brushy water source. At regular resting or watering places there are generally a number of pits worn in the ground. These are dusting holes and often will have feathers in them. Quail use the same areas for dusting day after day. When hunting, look for dusting areas and if the holes are fresh and have new feathers, the birds will be close by.

By late afternoon, the birds start getting restless and work their way back to the feeding grounds. Before dusk, the birds are in the neighborhood of the roosting cover. By sundown, the covey is safe high above ground in their roosting site.

Quail don't feed in the open, and where they feed depends upon where the cover is. The placement of brushy cover is perhaps the most important component for a usable area. Feeding sites have to have cover close by for escape routes. Food and water sources and roosting sites all need adjoining cover so birds can move from one to the other freely. Quail usually make the journey from area to area on foot, even though they will fly short distances from place to place.

I hunted several seasons in a canyon next to an apple orchard some miles from my home in Washington. I knew this bunch of birds by their first names. This covey I watched more than hunted. I'd been watching them at different times of the day, off and on all summer.

The hunting season had not opened yet. It was early morning and I was walking in the orchard toward the canyon. Fall was in the air. Bright Red Delicious apples weighed down the trees. Long wooden poles supported the horizontal limbs of the apple trees. A few apples lay on the ground. I picked one up, polished it on my shirt and bit down. Juice squirted out both sides of my mouth. I took a couple more bites and threw it down.

I often fly-fished a nearby stream. If fishing was slow, I took a break and visited my canyon covey. They were always around, but where they were depended on the time of day. The birds roosted on the western side of the canyon in a bunch of crabapple trees on a small knoll, surrounded with common sagebrush. After the sun peeked over the canyon wall the birds flew down and ventured out into the sage. A few started to the bottom of the canyon, others lingered, chasing in and out of openings in the sagebrush.

A trickle of water flowed through the canyon. Heavy brush and willows lined the rocky creek bed. A few birds stopped and drank. Others scurried across the open creek. Ten-foot weeds formed a large protective cover over the sparse, open ground. The birds ran up the hillside and into the tall weeds.

I walked into the canyon and worked my way up the eastern side of a gradual slope. Halfway up I sat down and listened to the valley quail calling. *Oh-HI-oh, oh-HI-oh.* I watched them fly down, cross the creek and begin feeding below me in the tall weeds, scratching like chickens.

An hour and a half went by. It was time to go fishing. I stood; a few birds close to me flushed and flew to the creek bottom, but most ran along the side of the hill and out of sight.

A week later I was sitting on the west side of the canyon above the crabapple trees. The sun was low but still warmed my back. The first bird appeared, a male. He crossed the creek. More followed. I watched them come up the hill toward the roost.

Once you scatter a covey of valley quail, singles hold tight.

Sometimes all of the birds walked to the trees, other times they flew from the bottom of the canyon to the roost trees. I believe when birds are feeding late they will fly to the roost rather than walk. Usually valley quail will roost on a western slope if a roosting site is available, especially during cold weather, to take advantage of the morning sun.

After loud whirling of many wings and a rustling of leaves, all was quiet on the western slope. The birds had settled in for the night and the only thing I heard was the trickle of the creek.

I have learned more about how and where to find valley quail from this one single covey than any other. This knowledge I use for hunting other coveys and I apply the same strategy to find other species of quail. I also do a lot of preseason scouting. Finding good quail habitat before the season can improve one's hunting immensely.

HUNTING VALLEY QUAIL

According to most western sportsmen, valley quail are in a class by themselves. They are sporty and when flushed explode with a roar of wings. Quail rise rapidly from the ground, level out to a diagonal height of about 15 feet and fly a relatively direct flight to cover. Most flights are between 100 and 300 yards, but I'm sure the distance a bird flies is determined by the cover and best escape route.

On two occasions I checked the speed of a valley quail while driving. On a level course I clocked one bird at 42 and another at 48 miles an hour. Some birds seem to fly much faster than this, but the speed can be exaggerated by the deceiving whirl of wings. As for a running speed, I clocked a quail in front of the pickup at about 15 miles per hour, but the bird was zigzagging.

To enjoy upland game hunting to the fullest there are two essential ingredients. One is to know their origin, distribution, life cycle, behavior, habitat, food, water and daily routine. The second: a trained bird dog is essential, be it a pointing dog, a flushing dog or a retriever. Most valley quail shooting involves birds flying into brushy or high cover. Quail are killed over dense cover and it takes a dog to find dead or crippled birds. Without a dog, too many birds are lost in the field.

I have hunted valley quail over a Labrador and will get to that story later. But my preference is the pointing breeds. When properly trained, they are also excellent retrievers.

A gun dog is important when hunting valley quail, especially for locating downed birds.

When hunting valley quail, a good bird dog is indispensable, even though some inexperienced pointing dogs may have difficulty handling a large covey of running birds.

Valley quail are fast flyers but generally move only a short distance after flushing and are easily found again. The fact is, with good scenting condition, pointers are deadly at pointing singles. After a covey is broken up they act much the same as bobwhite quail, and singles are almost impossible to find without a dog. Just seeing a properly trained pointer, running full speed into a slight breeze, suddenly slam into a staunch point, almost lifting its back legs off the ground, or a far-off retrieve of a crippled quail within a deep draw full of weeds will be remembered long after the smoke has cleared the shotgun barrels. To me, hunting quail, or any upland game bird for that matter, without a dog is like watching a football game with only one team on the field. Nothing exciting happens.

About Running Coveys: If the topography is rolling hills, this usually means hunting uphill or along a draw. I hunt for quail with two or three pointing dogs. I have Brittanys, English pointers and an English setter. I let my dogs run big and when a large covey is scented the dogs slow to a crawl. This gives me an opportunity to figure out what the birds are doing. At the first approach of danger, valley quail run. A hunter cannot keep up with running birds, but a dog can. My dogs keep working the birds, actually following them. It may be down a draw or up a side hill. Keep in mind, valley quail are unquestionably good runners, so it is important to get the dogs in a position to either hold the birds or flush the whole bunch.

Valley quail generally have several methods of escape when pressed by dogs. First is to sit tight in very heavy woody cover, so the dogs have to rout them out. Second, they sneak off and run, following any overhead cover available. If this happens, let the dogs keep working them until the birds flush. Third, the birds will run a short distance and then flush straight away from the dogs. This is ideal. Fourth, they'll run at a right angle from the dogs. If this happens, let the dogs follow the birds and flush them. When they flush, the birds may wheel off, passing the hunter, which can result in some fine wingshooting. Every one of these escape methods is extremely rapid and can confuse even the most seasoned dog or hunter.

*Hunting valley quail with a Labrador retriever is how
Dave Zalunardo does it, and as a team they are efficient.*

Many times, all the birds will gather in one spot. I use three or four big-running dogs to find them. I hunt valley quail in big country so I encourage my dogs to range far. As winter approaches, food quantity and cover shrink and coveys join together. These large groups can contain as many as 100 birds. Large flocks have a better chance for survival but when broken up will lie well for a pointing dog.

Once the dogs have scented and pointed the birds, a large covey will usually run, but my dogs will slow up and point until I get there. When I arrive the pointers automatically relocate following the strongest scent of the running birds. I walk slowly, circling the area and let the dogs work the singles and small groups that have scattered. Even if the valley quail do flush after the dogs point several times, which happens often, the covey will scatter after landing.

This is the time when more than one dog is important and the real pointing begins. After the birds have scattered and land, many will run a short distance. Some will hide individually; others will form small groups and hide together. Give the birds time to lay down scent before pursuing them. It's also important, once a bird is found, to cover the rest of the ground thoroughly, starting with a small circle and enlarging it as you go. If the dogs only find a few birds, I encourage the dogs to cover the same ground over and over again.

If a covey flushes and stays in a tight group they will reassemble quickly and run. My strategy then is go after the covey as soon as possible. After the next flush, if the birds still stay in a tight group I do the same. Once the birds scatter, as I said before, I wait a few minutes and have the dogs comb the same area over and over again. This usually brings results. After the birds are scattered, valley quail hunting is at its best, and this is when knowing the birds is important.

When I hunt new country, I survey the terrain before I put any dogs on the ground. I look closely at the habitat and try to judge where the birds will be hanging out that particular time of day. Are the birds feeding, resting, loafing or picking gravel? During early morning and late afternoon valley quail feed frequently on greens out in the open areas of low cover. As the day warms up and the sun is high, coveys seek out some type of overhead canopy close to heavy cover. This may be tall trees or shrubs with little ground cover beneath the canopy so the birds can move about and still have good escape routes to heavier cover.

As I survey the country I also listen. Valley quail are quite vocal and while feeding can be heard a long way off. There are times I've used a quail call and have located a covey, but I find a call more useful after a covey is scattered. If valley quail have been hunted often in a particular area, I recommend being as quiet as possible while listening or calling. Loud voices or slamming hunting rig doors stop them from calling.

When a covey is found look carefully at the habitat itself, then the placement of the different types of cover, and try to figure out why the birds are there. This knowledge can be useful in finding new coveys.

The habits of the valley quail vary with the weather and seasons. On warm days, singles hold tightly and seldom run. If the day is wet or rainy, valley quail have a tendency to run after landing and singles may flush wild. In wet conditions, a flushed covey, instead of flying to heavy ground cover, will fly to thickets with little understory and run to avoid getting wet.

All quail are gregarious and need to assemble as soon as danger has passed. I believe it's in the best interest of the quail and the quail hunter not to scatter a covey late in the day. After dark, small groups will not covey up and are more vulnerable to predators and other hazards. Nor should a covey of quail be broken up on several consecutive days. Once a covey of birds is found, scattered and hunted, let the birds reassemble and be unmolested for several days. Small fragmented groups of any kind of quail are almost impossible to hunt, and it's in the best interest of the hunters not to hunt them. On well-managed Southern plantations, wild quail are never hunted over the same course day after day, and the same should be true when hunting Western quail.

Labs and Quail: I'm willing to bet that we agree that there are very few outdoor experiences more enjoyable than chasing after upland game birds. The sight of a large covey of valley quail running across a sandy coulee or flushing from a draw and scattering on a hillside gets our undivided attention. But add a dog, and the sport sharpens our senses and quickens our instincts.

I have a kennel full of pointing dogs, but Dave Zalunardo has Labrador retrievers, the most popular hunting breed in North America. So why not use them for hunting quail? That's what Dave does with his Labrador retriever, Chuck, and with good results.

A large covey of valley quail will give any hunting dog fits. But that does not bother Dave or his Lab—both have the birds figured out. The routine is simple: Dave knows the birds' habits and the habitat. He casts his dog and the retriever does the rest, working methodically ahead of the hunter. Once the dog finds fresh quail scent, he slowly follows the moving birds with Dave right behind him.

The sight of a big retriever working the cover, shaking down every bush is well worth the muddy paw prints on the kitchen floor. It may take several hundred yards before the dog is close enough to flush the covey. Many times, some of the birds even flush within shooting range. Once the covey is scattered, though, the birds hold tight and the Lab goes to work flushing the singles and doubles. This is when the real fun begins.

The find, the flush, the shot, the retrieve, a plump ball of feathers and, after a day's hunting, a superb meal of wild quail with a big black dog curled up under the table is what bird hunting is all about.

Bird of Brushy Cover: Critics past and present have given the hunting of valley quail a bum rap. Some have said valley quail always congregate in large flocks and cannot be approached within shotgun range. Others have said the bird is a notorious runner, rarely flies, coveys cannot be broken up, and can't be worked with pointing dogs. Some even say the valley quail is much too small a target and not worth shooting. I would have to agree that valley quail do form large flocks, can be notorious runners and are a small target. However, I highly disagree that they aren't worth hunting and aren't for pointing dogs.

There was no reason to quicken my pace. Looking left, I kept an eye on both of my hunting partners. They pushed hard through the dry, chest-high tangled tumbleweed, stalled years past by the brambles. The large, curled blackberry leaves with bright streaks of reds and greens clung tenuously to the vines, falling as the hunters brushed past. The men moved toward the sounds of the dogs' beepers. The high-pitched beeps indicated two dogs on point. The sounds came from the center of the large briar patch, beneath the high cover. The pointers were not visible. Holding their guns high, the going was rough for the two hunters. Shooting, or even seeing the quail flush, would have been a long shot, but someone had to get to the dogs on point.

Of all the game birds native to the west, none is more enjoyable to hunt than valley quail.

On my side was a long, narrow row of tall prairie cottonwoods strung along a wide irrigation ditch. Along both sides of the trees, high pigweed stripped of foliage had dropped its shining, circular seeds on the ground. Good food for valley quail and a ideal place to find them, I thought. It seemed to me the only departure for the birds would be through the trees, but even if the quail flew out on my side, getting a shot off would be questionable.

The sound changed to a roar of wings made by a large covey flush of quail, but no shots were fired. The silence was broken once again by the dogs chasing through the heavy brush in the direction of the birds. The quail simply flew low toward the trees, made a sharp turn to the left, followed the ditch for about 30 yards, crossed the creek, continued up the hill, fanned out, and landed on a small, flat bench full of bunchgrass and sagebrush. Above the spot where the birds landed was a steep, rocky ridge 200 yards away. I reasoned we couldn't walk above them, but they also could not go over the top without flying.

While waiting for the two hunters to join me, I watched the hill for any movement of birds. The two hunters crashed though the heavy brush, crossed the ditch and then the creek to my side. By the time the three of us assembled and laid out a strategy to approach the scattered birds, the dogs were already on point 30 yards below where the main bunch of birds landed. A soft wind blew over the ridge. The breeze seemed to flow down the rocky outcropping, following the contour of the steep slope passing through the sagebrush flat where the covey put in, and it carried the scent of the birds to the dogs below. The pointers were motionless against a backdrop of waving, harvest-gold bunchgrass and purple sage. The three of us moved up the hill, slowly passing the dogs. We had 'em pinned down.

Today more and more people are hunting western upland game birds. Of all the game birds native to the west coast of United States, none is more enjoyable or appreciated than the valley quail.

Chapter Three
GAMBEL'S QUAIL

The cheerful three-noted call of the male Gambel's quail is a characteristic sound of the southwestern deserts and the soundtrack of Western movies: con-CHi-ta, con-CHi-ta, con-CHi-ta.

Arizona: Think Arizona: land of the Navajo, javelina, gila monster — a place where saguaro cactus take root. Sportsmen come hundreds of miles to shoot Arizona's most popular game bird, the Gambel's quail, and thousands of acres of public land make this resource available to all.

It was January. The sun was warm this time of year and the desert air smelled of cactus candy — sweet, tart. The Toyota pickup was parked off Highway 93. I heard a vehicle go by now and then, but I was far enough off the main road to exercise my two Brittanys.

I was surrounded by cholla, yucca, saguaro, crucifixion thorn and Joshua trees, all unfriendly. Shoe and McGillie wouldn't leave the dirt road that's blazed through the cacti desert. I was thumbing through the *North America Field Guide To The Southwest*, looking up saguaro cactus. It was the first I'd ever seen. I read that the saguaro (pronounced sah-wah'-ro) is the state flower of Arizona and is protected by law. It grows very slowly and lives over 200 years. It has the capacity to store large quantities of water and flowers each year regardless of drought. The flower opens at night and is visited by nectar-feeding insects and bats. The fruit was an important food for native Americas in that region and the woody ribs of the stems were used for building shelters.

I was back on the highway. The sun was heating up and both windows were half open. The saguaro cacti were sentinels guarding the blacktop. I stopped in Wickenburg for lunch, looked at a road map to see how many more miles to my destination. I figured I should get there before dusk. Driving this straight stretch of highway, all the scenery looked the same—cactus, cactus, and more cactus. I wondered if Willcox, Arizona, would have the same desert habitat. Jeff left word at the motel to meet him at home. The next morning I was heading out of town. I stopped at the supermarket and handed the young girl my driver's license and asked for a non-resident bird hunting permit. Then I asked how far to Bowie. Little over 20 miles she said. I picked up stuff for lunch.

I met Jeff at Dan Bailey's fly shop in Livingston, Montana, when he was attending his first year of collage at Montana State University. When he returned the following year, we spent several weeks fishing some of the famous rivers in the West. In return, he invited me to bird hunt in his home state. Twenty years have passed since then.

Before college, Jeff kicked around between Willcox and Safford and worked as a farm hand and a cowboy. There

weren't many places Jeff couldn't get on, even though much of the land is public. At that time Jeff had no interest in hunting but knew the country and had seen quail while working. After hunting Huns in Montana and seeing my Brittanys, he thought it would be a blast to hunt Gambel's quail with pointing dogs.

Jeff put his new 20-gauge over-under Browning Citori and his hunting vest in the extra-cab and jumped in the front seat. I backed out of the yard and he told me to drive the frontage road, then to turn right on the next dirt road.

"We'll stay on backcountry roads all the way to Safford. I'll show you desert country and agricultural land, and point out where quail have been in the past," he explained.

The desert habitat here looked a lot different than the saguaro forest I drove through the day before. There were still plenty of thorny plants out there, but I believed the dogs could run this country without boots.

"Ben, turn right here. I worked several miles down this sandy lane. This time of year the fields are cut, but all the ditches and corners are brushy and full of windblown tumbleweed. When I cut these fields, quail were in the

Ben Brown approaches his pointing Brittany slowly anticipating a flush of Gambel's quail.

weedy places," Jeff explained.

"Are there any scaled quail here?" I asked.

"You mean cotton tops? That's what we call them here."

"Yes," I said, "cotton tops. This doesn't look like Gambel's quail country. I thought they were more a desert bird."

"I believe you're right, Ben. This all used to be desert, but when irrigation became available, farmers plowed parts of it up. This whole area is a patchwork of desert and croplands. Farmers cannot get water everywhere. Some areas are too low and other places too high, so there is lots of land that isn't tilled and that's where the birds live. Down this lane are grassy hills and I have seen a covey of cotton tops cross the road there. But here I've only seen Gambel's."

"Stop here for a moment, Ben." Jeff pointed out the window of the truck. "This big corner is about 300 acres. The trees and brush that run through the middle are sub-irrigated. In summer, groundwater seeps into the low areas. The trees have grown a lot since I've worked here. When the fields are cut, weeds blow up against the fence rows and into the corners. Most of it is tumbleweed. It's good quail food,

but hard to walk through."

A good part of the morning we spent looking at different covers. After a while, I wondered aloud why we didn't go back and hunt the big corner. I also suggested the dogs needed to get out.

Jeff was silent for some time, then spoke suddenly. "Let's turn around and hunt the big corner. It's as good a place to start as any. In the past, I've always seen birds there."

When we left Jeff's house, there was not a cloud in the sky nor a breath of wind. Now the wind was kicking up and dust from the plowed field was blowing in our faces. I stood behind the pickup rustling the dogs, trying to get bells on them. Jeff was holding his shotgun and my 20-gauge Belgium Browning lightning superposed shotgun.

The dogs were on the ground and in a minute or less, a quail called. I had never heard a Gambel's quail call in the wild but remember the old B-rated Western movies, when the Indians were crawling on their bellies and had the star cowboy boxed in a deep canyon. The movie intensified and the only sound came from the desert background, *con-CHi-ta, con-CHi-ta*, a desert quail.

We looked at each other and Jeff said, "Gambel's quail."

I loaded the 20-gauge shotgun and my adrenaline told me to hurry, but I didn't. The two dogs broke through the head-high tumbleweeds stacked up at the edge of the cut field. The wind flung a couple of tumbleweeds over a dog's head and into a lone mesquite tree. They hung there like unlighted lanterns as we passed. A quail flushed out from the top of the mesquite tree.

Jeff shouted, "Gambel's!" It flew towards a long row of tangled tumbleweed, creosote brush, mesquite and willows. "Must be one of the birds that called," he said.

Shoe and McGillie ran across an open sand dune, dodging prickly pear and large clumps of beargrass and yucca, then dropped out of sight into the shallow brushy draw. A single bird called again. Tracks lead into the thicket. "Quail tracks," I called to Jeff,

I no longer heard the dog bells. Jeff and I walked to the edge of the tree-lined thicket. The thicket had little understory. Both dogs were visible 20 yards away, but the tangle of brush and low trees were impregnable. I called the dogs but they wouldn't move.

Jeff and I split up. At the first opening, I tried to get to the dogs and flush the birds. I struggled as willow branches slapped me in the face. Finally, I broke through to the other side. The dogs followed the scent to the opening and slowly moved down the line of heavy cover in Jeff's direction.

Just as Jeff stepped into the open, a huge covey of quail flushed. The birds flew toward a mesquite-shrub-grassland savanna ahead of us. I marked them down, looked at Jeff and he was pointing a finger toward the birds. He also had them marked.

By the time we reached the end of the savanna another large covey was found. Both of our game bags were bulging at the bottom. Hunting all morning back and forth in the savanna, we could feel the heat cutting the light breeze.

We turned back and followed an old irrigation ditch that ran along the plowed field. I was thinking we might put up a few singles from the two scattered coveys on the way back to the hunting rig, but the dogs seemed tired and walked in front of us in the open field.

When we reached the pickup, it was long past lunchtime. I removed the Gambel's quail from my vest and lay them backside down on the tailgate of the pickup. Jeff did the same.

"Let's have a look at the difference between the Gambel's and its close cousin the valley quail," I said to to my hunting partner. I opened to page 91, plate 22 of *Peterson's Field Guide To The Western Birds* and looked at the colored drawings.

The Gambel's quail has a black-plumed headdress that identifies it in its desert kingdom.

The identification markings in the book pointed out the breast of the desert quail is without the scaling that is so noticeable a part of the valley quail's markings. Both of us examined a female and male Gambel's quail, looking at the distinctive belly markings. As I looked at the pair of quail in my hand, I said to Jeff, "To the hunter who studies and thoroughly knows the birds that he hunts, the two can hardly be confused."

In the book, all of the quail are displayed on one page. Jeff said, "Some hunters say the Gambel's is the handsomest of the all the quail, but for those who have hunted all six North American species that must be a hard call."

A couple of years later I hunted with another friend in an agricultural area similar to the surroundings Jeff and I hunted. But that was the last time. Since then I hunt the unscarred desert landscapes within view of working windmills, the prairie skyscrapers of the Southwest.

KNOWING THE BIRD

Gambel's Quail Origins: In the 1840s, naturalist William Gambel collected plant and animal specimens in the Southwest and named this fine bird. Little did he know there are seven subspecies and each has slight color variations due to their regional residence. The differences are so slight that it is almost impossible for an untrained eye to identify one subspecies from another.

The Gambel's quail (*Lophortyx gambelii*) and the valley quail (*Lophortyx californicus*) are closely related and look alike. Both belong to the same order, family, and genus and are very similar in size, appearance and habits.

There is some question that all of the birds' distribution today is historic range. Thousands of Gambel's quail were trapped and relocated in and out of the birds' native range. It is not clear how successful the restocking of Gambel's quail has been. Today if the birds' habitat has not been destroyed, the present and the original range are about the same.

Even though the distribution of the valley quail has been widely extended by restocking and transplantation, the Gambel's quail range has not. Today the birds' range does overlap a small area of southern California, but this overlapping is really more a meandering line than a straight border. Both species occur on this fragmented border, but there are also two different habitats that intermingle, and each species uses a different type of habitat. The climate and vegetation and the birds' use of it is really what determines their adapted native range. The big difference between Gambel's quail and valley quail is their very different environments.

DISTRIBUTION

The Gambel's quail is indigenous to the Sonoran Desert and the Grassland/Chihuahuan deserts scrub. This desert quail's historical range is the desert regions of southern California, southern Nevada, Arizona, New Mexico and northern Mexico. The Gambel's quail range in some areas also overlaps that of the scaled quail, the Mearns' quail and the endangered masked bobwhite. In overall distribution, the Gambel's and the scaled quail have about the same amount of range per square mile in the United States. The overlap of these two species occurs along the southern borders of Arizona and New Mexico. If you want both species on a single hunting trip, this is the place to go.

With the exception of Utah and California, I have hunted Gambel's quail in the other states in which they live. I recommend Arizona as there is more accessible public lands available to bird hunt. Gambel's quail is the state's most popular game bird and the hunting opportunities are unlimited.

IN THE BUSH, IN THE HAND

In medieval times knights in armor had different-colored plumed helmets to identify their local fiefdom. Gambel's quail have a black-plumed headdress to identify them in their desert kingdom. In spring, a male Gambel's quail will perch high on a velvet mesquite tree, its branches ablaze with 3-inch candles of pale yellow catkins. His call rings across the cacti wilderness, a proposal to a female or a challenge to any rival male.

When an intruding male approaches, the defender goes forth to do battle. There is a skirmish even though it does not amount to much. The defender is usually the undisputed victor and returns to his domain. The Gambel's quail starts calling again. Finally, a hen inconspicuously moves in and walks under the male's mesquite castle. He flies down, struts around, bobbing his black-plumed helmet. This is his courtship dance and soon the hen is mated. Gambel's quail are monogamous and choose one female during the breeding season.

The Gambel's quail is more vocal than other quail. When moving or feeding, the whole covey keeps in contact

Approximate range of the Gambel's quail.

with one another. The calls of the Gambel's quail have a metallic ring, notes are varied and higher pitched then the valley quail. The "crow" of the Gambel's, while similar to the valley quail, has two additional notes at the end and a great deal softer tone. An unusual characteristic of the Gambel's is that when flushed the birds sometimes make a sort of a soft screeching cackle. Gambel's, being very vocal, will answer a hunter's call quite readily, even if it is poorly executed.

The adult Gambel's quail is about 11 inches long, weighs 6 ounces and has a wingspan of 12 inches. The bird's most striking characteristic is its topknot. His plume is black and club-shaped, curved over the forehead and is much heavier and longer than the valley quail's topknot. Its eyes and beak are black. The male's crown is reddish-brown, bordered by a white line. The throat and sides of the head are black with a white border. The back of the neck cape is steel gray. The bird's back, rump, wings and tail are grayish-brown. Below the wings, the sides and flanks are reddish-brown with white streaks. The feet and legs are a steely gray-black.

The adult female is pale in color and overall is grayer than the male. She does not have a black throat and head, nor the white lines.

The most distinguishing differences between the Gambel's and the valley quail is that the Gambel's lower breast-belly feathers are yellowish and in the middle area there is a large black spot.

LIFE CYCLE AND BEHAVIOR

Gambel's quail remain in winter flocks until about mid-March, then begin to pair up. The height of the mating season occurs mid-April until early May. Do above-normal rains help Gambel's quail? The answers is yes, if they come at the right time of year, and no, if they don't. Of the three species of quail that live in the Southwest, the Gambel's quail lives in the lowest elevation, which is much dryer and warmer. Gambel's quail are also the first to nest and early rain is essential to bring off a brood.

To have a good reproductive year, Gambel's quail need rain in January or February. Winter rains are needed to produce green vegetation for quail in the spring. Studies have shown greens are essential for active breeding and good quail reproduction. Nesting is early and there are more birds in breeding condition when conditions are favorable.

In years with no rain during the winter months, fewer birds are in breeding condition and nesting is extended. In extremely dry years, many Gambel's quail will terminate their partnership or not pair up at all.

During good productive years, the peak of the hatch is in mid-April to May. During unfavorable years, hatching can be as late as August and September. If the first nest is lost the hen will renest, but the number of eggs is usually less. Because the desert is so hot in the summer, a third nest is very unlikely. When dry conditions occur, broods are hatched over a longer time span and young birds in the field are of different ages. Also, if a hen does renest and brings off a brood, these chicks are much younger than the birds hatched during the peak season. Seeing different age groups in the field does not mean that a hen has double clutched. Gambel's quail bringing off two broods in a season is highly unlikely due to the harsh desert environment.

The success of the hatch is what determines the number of birds going into the fall hunting season. A large carryover of birds following a good hatching year can help the next year's population of birds going in to the nesting season.

The female Gambel's quail makes her nest on the ground. It is generally a shallow depression under a mesquite or some shrub. The nest lining is made of dried grass, weeds and a few feathers. The average clutch of eggs is about a dozen, but in dry years the number of eggs will be less.

The male does not incubate the eggs but stays in the vicinity of the nest during incubation and is alert for danger and attentive to the hen. Like the valley quail, if the hen is killed, some males will take over her duties and incubate the eggs and care for the chicks.

Incubation takes about 22 days. As soon as the last chick is hatched, both adults lead the chicks away from the nest. Like other members of the quail family, chicks can run soon after hatching. The adults search out safe places for the birds to feed. For several days the chicks entire diet is animal matter. From the very first day, the young are extremely talented at catching insects.

Both parents use calls to communicate with the young. These calls are important in keeping the chicks together as a single unit. At the first sign of any danger, the hen gives a warning call and her chicks hide and can disappear in open cover. When the brood is out of harm's way, she calls again to let the chicks know the danger has passed.

Young birds can fly a short distance by the time they are 10 days old. During the first several weeks the adults direct the chicks to all their daily activities. After hatching, the hen broods her chicks at night, but that lasts only a short time. The desert stays quite warm at night, and within a week or two young birds roost in low bushes close to the adults.

As long as the young birds need attention, the brood stays close together. As the birds grow older, they become much stronger flyers and more independent. At eight to nine weeks the young are half grown and can move as fast as the adults. Gambel's quail prefer to run from danger but will fly if necessary. As winter approaches, the juveniles go through molting changes and are fully-grown with adult plumage by 16 weeks. When grown, the Gambel's quail are strong runners and depend largely on their legs for travel, but when pressed hard will choose to fly.

Once a large covey of birds is spotted on the ground, pursue them slowly. Running birds divide into smaller groups and this is where a dog can work a splinter group and point singles.

HABITAT

The Gambel's quail lives in a harsh but beautiful country. Generally speaking, it's a bird of the brushy desert and thorny forest, places full of mesquite, cholla, yucca, cactus, and other plants unfriendly to those who trespass. The one plant that seems to be associated with this quail is the mesquite. Even though mesquite is not essential to the bird as sagebrush is to sage grouse, these two species share much of the the same range.

Nine species of mesquite are native to North America, but the true quail bushes are the velvet and honey mesquite, which are widely distributed in Gambel's quail country. There are some interesting facts about these two species. The honey mesquite is a large shrub or small tree and associated with sandy soils. In very windy areas mesquite trees become buried and only the ends of the branches are exposed. This is the tree that the indigenous peoples were referring to when they spoke of digging for wood.

The velvet mesquite is a tree, but when growing together or when young, it is shrub-like. The native Americans used the velvet mesquite pods for food and the wood for fuel. Today large mesquite trees are sought not only for wood-fuel for cooking, but also for quality furniture.

Desert thickets along rivers, creeks, arroyos, draws and sand washes are good Gambel's quail hangouts. Not only mesquite, but ironwood, catclaw, saguaro, prickly pear, coffeeberry, hackberry and several scrub oaks are all good indicators of quail habitat. Saltbrush, creosote brush, skunkbush, rabbit brush, brittle bush and snakeweed make up some of the low-growing plant communities in which the Gambel's quail live.

Gambel's quail use dense scrub regions of the desert. These places are generally in the vicinity of desert windmills, watering holes and springs, though this water can be several miles away. Gambel's quail are reluctant to travel any great distance if good shrub cover is not available. The water source has to have highways of cover usable for the birds' other daily needs. Birds will also use brushy slopes, fields of cholla cactus and rocky sidehills to feed as long as there is thick cover close by or within these areas.

Mesquite in many areas has recolonized in grasslands and competes for space, water and light. Much of this recolonization is due to overgrazing because there is no fuel for fire and burning is one way to control mesquite in grasslands. When grasslands are dominated by mesquite, many ranchers eradicate the plant.

Gambel's quail do not fly far, and hit the ground running to look for the best cover to hide.

A mesquite savanna is beneficial for wildlife and livestock. Scattered trees provide shade for birds and animals, and grass remains greener longer under a canopy of cover. Gambel's are associated with forested edges or islands within mesquite savannas. Semi-desert grasslands, open chaparral communities, and riparian cover that is scrub-invaded also have Gambel's quail.

FOOD AND WATER

The diet of the Gambel's quail is similar to other quail. Gambel's quail diet is made up of 65 percent green succulent vegetation, thirty percent seeds and grains, and five percent animal matter. In winter and spring, Gambel's quail feed primarily on greens. Their most important foods are the greens and seeds of annuals such as deervetch, filaree and legumes of the locoweed and lupine families. Legumes are the most important group of plants consumed by Gambel's quail. In spring, the flowers and leaves of mesquite and other legumes are the birds' best source of food. If good rains occur early in the year, the desert becomes alive with many succulent plants and greens are numerous. When forbs become available in the spring, they are also an important food source throughout the birds' range.

Even though the adult Gambel's quail is primarily a vegetarian, for the first few weeks of a chicks life, it depends on animal foods, primarily insects. After several weeks, young birds are also feeding on succulent plants, fruits and seeds as they become available.

In summer greens are not as succulent and are less accessible, so the Gambel's quail diet is mostly fruits and seeds. Woody plants provide much of the Gambel's quail's diet in summer and fall when they feed on dry seeds, fruits and seeds of fruits. Many common summer fruits in the desert are used, such as the fruits of the cholla, prickly pear and several other cacti. Mesquite fruit and seeds are probably the most widely used. A large number of other desert plants furnish seeds in the late summer and fall.

Some areas of the Southwestern desert are irrigated or have dry-land farming. Birds that live next to these farmlands feed on many planted crops. Seeds of wheat, oats, barley and corn are all used for feed by quail in summer and fall. Cultivated truck crops and pastures such as flax, sweet clover, alfalfa, and lettuce are also eaten by quail. Where there is farming there are weeds. A large percentage of the Gambel's diet around cultivated fields is weed seeds. Pigweed, chickweed, wild sunflower and Russian thistle (tumbleweed) are eaten during the fall and winter.

Semi-desert scrub grasslands and desert savannas have a mix of woody plants, shrubs, herbs and grass. This combination provides all of the birds' seasonal food needs such as animal matter, greens, fruits and seeds.

The availability of water for Gambel's quail in some years is important, but not to the extent that it is for valley quail. Weather is directly related to the condition of the birds' habitat. The need for Gambel's quail to use open water for drinking is tied directly to the amount of moisture that is available in plants. When succulent greens are available Gambel's quail use little free water. When there is little rain, the water supply and the food supply both suffer. Succulent plants, vegetable foods, and insects all become less abundant.

One last thought about water—when I hunt Gambel's quail, I look for places that have water. It may be a stream, a desert windmill, a tank, watering holes or a spring. In dry years birds are generally found in the vicinity of some type of open water. I have found that Gambel's quail travel farther than one might think for water; however I have found the best population of birds exists where there is a beneficial supply of food, water and cover. But I'm not saying that places without water don't have birds, however.

DAILY ROUTINE

The daily movements of Gambel's quail depend on the availability of succulent vegetation or water and the food supply. If the two are in close proximity, birds do not have to travel. But if not, they will spend more time traveling throughout the day.

The home range of a covey of Gambel's quail can be as small as 25 acres to over 100 acres. (A square mile is 640 acres.) Most covey movement is less than 500 yards. Seasonal variations of the food supply are closely associated with the birds' distance of travel. When food is in short supply several coveys may overlap and can be found in rich food areas. The seasonal movements for a covey are less than a mile. Gambel's quail do not migrate or have seasonal shifts in elevation. During years of extreme drought, birds will expand their range, but no farther than necessary.

Gambel's quail are most active early in the morning, feeding, drinking or looking for succulent vegetation. The feeding period is about two hours, unless the weather if foul and then the feeding period is extended. Once feeding is over, much of the day is spent dust-bathing, picking grit or resting in a convenient place in thick cover.

Gambel's quail feed again later in the day. Before sunset the birds work their way to a roosting site. Many times the birds will use the same area to roost, but rarely use the exact location they used the night before. Gambel's quail fly up to their to roosting site.

Gambel's quail move from feeding to drinking to loafing places on foot. In many areas of their range the soil is sandy. A large covey of quail can make a lot of tracks in the sand. Each species of Western quail has a different walking pattern. Gambel's quail do not seem to travel as much in single file as do valley or scaled quail. Gambel's quail spread out over a considerable area when traveling or feeding, whereas scaled quail walk and feed in a much tighter regiment.

One of my favorite places to hunt Gambel's quail is a tree-lined arroyo. On both sides is shrub grasslands. The arroyo runs for miles; stock tanks and windmills are far and few. Gambel's and scaled quail both use the water tanks. Tracks are everywhere, leading to the water source. Quail highways I call them. If you look carefully you can tell the difference between the two kinds of quail, not only by birds' foot patterns, but also by the direction the birds are coming from, in the kind of habitat each species uses. Finding tracks of Western quail gives me more information of the birds' whereabouts than any other single factor. Watering places can leave telltale signs of footprints. If there are no tracks, there are no birds, and I leave the area.

HUNTING GAMBEL'S QUAIL

The Gambel's quail is the most important game bird in the southwestern United States and northwestern Mexico. This native birds' popularity in the desert country is equal to the bobwhite in the Midwest and South.

The Gambel's quail is a fast little target and can give any upland bird hunter some real shooting thrills. Surely this is some of the best wingshooting the West has to offer, but you may also find yourself gripped by a real passion for the breathtaking desert. In the morning, the low light is magical as it casts long shadows across the cacti-studded landscape. During midday when the sun is high, the desert has a beauty that is wrapped in loneliness. Evening takes on a golden light that softens the harshness of the sun and transforms the desert into a world of loveliness.

87

Ben Brown's Brittany collects a plump Gambel's quail after he dumps it in a patch of mesquite.

When a big flock (50 to 60) of Gambel's quail is seen and pursued, the birds will divide and the hunter usually follows the largest bunch. As the birds are followed farther, the birds will divide again and again. This process of dividing continues as long as the birds are on the ground.

Two important maneuvers have to be executed: one is when a large covey of birds is found they have to be pursued slowly; the second is a hunter cannot keep up with a running covey of birds, so a dog is needed. As the dog works the scent, the running birds divide into smaller groups. The pointer can only work one splinter group at a time and eventually may point just a single bird. This is when the hunter should circle, walking slowly in order for the dog to find the rest of the scattered birds.

I have found that the same hunting tactics I use for valley quail work for Gambel's quail. Even though the ground cover in the desert is more open, my dogs work Gambel's quail quite well.

The use of pointing dogs in the arid desert country of the southwestern states was relatively new when I started hunting Gambel's quail. This dry, hot country of cactus, snakes, gila monsters and javelinas was thought to be too hostile for any hunting dog. But then again, hazards for dogs are everywhere — from roadways to rattlesnakes.

A hunter has to have confidence in his pointing dogs' ability to hunt any new species of game bird. Most pointers adapt quite well to desert quail, but the biggest disadvantage for the dog in desert country is poor scenting conditions much of the hunting year. The dry, sandy soil, heat and the lack of humidity in this arid country are the main factors that contribute to poor scenting for the dogs.

Give your pointer plenty of water — and often. Water stimulates a sensitive nose that helps the dog pick up fresh scent. The time of year and day are also big factors in helping the dog find birds. On some days, no time of day seems to work, but the rule I go by is if the weather forecast is for hot, dry weather and little air movement, I hunt early mornings and late afternoons. I find these time periods the most productive for good scenting conditions.

The time of year is also important for productive scenting conditions. No immature game bird lays down as much scent as older birds. I'm not sure why, but I do know this is the case. Maybe it's a young bird's defense mechanism or maybe it's the kind of food consumed during that time of year.

By mid-December, the weather is usually cooler. The

birds are mature, and hunting and scenting are better for the dogs. When scenting conditions are poor, a dog won't point as readily, though if there is little or no understory cover, some of my dogs have been known to sight point and will work the birds as if smelling them.

As a rule, when a large flock of desert quail is found, the birds must be scattered. After the birds are dispersed, an experienced hunter knows he's in for some great shooting. To the Western hunter there is nothing finer than working a pointing dog on a large, broken-up covey of tight-lying Gambel's for half an hour or so. It's the time when birds hold tight and a good dog earns his biscuit. This is also when the desert quail behaves much like his distant cousin, the bobwhite, and holds tight for your pointer and may flush unexpectedly, flying up your shirt sleeve.

Many hunters hesitate to use dogs in such tough country because of the abundance of cacti, but I don't! If the conditions warrant it, I use dog boots. Some dog people may disagree, but I like my dogs to break after the shot in order to find the downed bird as soon as possible. I realize this can be hazardous for a dog chasing a low-flying quail, but it's the hunter's responsibility not to shoot when the conditions aren't right for the dog. Bird hunting with pointing dogs is done in many ways and enjoyed for many different reasons.

Bird of the Singing Windmills: Even though Gambel's quail make excellent table fare, it seems to me they've always been hunted more for sport than food. Gambel's quail are wary runners, the coveys are explosive upon flushing, and are thereby a pleasure to hunt with pointing dogs.

It was a cool afternoon in January. The southern sky had mackerel clouds hanging over the isolated range of mountains, but we were headed in the opposite direction. Midday had been hot, but my partner Ben Brown and I had planned to hunt midday and our timing couldn't have been better. The weather was changing rapidly and looked more promising by the minute. The temperature was in the low 60s and dropping, with a moist breeze blowing. The wind seemed to follow the meandering arroyo and changed the tire tracks on the sandy road to snake-like ripples. Once out of the truck, the Brittanys pushed into the wind and disappeared into the tall rabbit brush, all of them out of view before Ben and I had our light 20-gauges uncased. Ben said the area had not been hunted this season and the reports he received from the ranch hands were promising.

Most of the cover was a soft amber color, but still unfriendly. The trees' green foliage was down and brown, but the rabbit brush still held its muted, pale green colors. We walked in the direction the dogs had gone, following the sandy road toward the singing windmill. The Brittanys found the water tank before Ben and I got there, their bellies dripping water as they crisscrossed the road.

As we were walking though the high cover, listening to the dog beepers, a single Gambel's quail got up out of the brush at my feet. I didn't mount the gun, but instead marked the bird down on the grassy hillside high above us. I could also see more quail dashing ahead of us on the ground. The Brittanys were pointing and running, pointing and running, their beepers changing to the pointing mode each time they stopped. We were into a large covey of running Gambel's quail.

There were quail tracks everywhere in the sand, and the dogs were in hot pursuit. After several staunch points, the dogs finally caught up to them, and the large bunch of running Gambel's rushed into the air with a tremendous roar of wings. They flew in the same direction as the single I had flushed.

I marked several birds down and saw others running up the hillside. The dogs knew the birds' approximate location, and by the time Ben and I walked up the hill they were locked up tight on point. Ben walked in on the first point and a quail got up and peeled off down the hill. At the shot, the bird tumbled and feathers drifted down, following the wind that hugged the contour of the rocky hill. Ben admired the bird for a while before he put it into his vest.

Between the two of us, we collected a bird or two more out of the covey then decided to look for a new bunch. We found a couple more coveys and took a few more birds. After circling around to the truck, Ben and I took a moment to appreciate these birds We smoothed their feathers and laid them down in a row, their topknot feathers casting long shadows on the sand.

Sycamore Canyon: There is a Sycamore Canyon near Williams, Arizona, but I have no link to that canyon or the town. The sycamore canyon I hunt is not its real name. The canyon is named after a family who homesteaded before the turn of the last century. It has a bit of history; Mexican banditos, outlaws and cattle rustlers. If sycamores could talk, I'm sure their ancestors would have a few hanging stories to tell. It was wild then and it still is today.

Water holes are premium in desert habitat.
Steve Smith waits for the author's dog to cool down.

Running through the center of the sycamores is a gentle, shallow arroyo. In January, the canyon's rubbled creek is covered with large, dry, star-shaped leaves that shade a lively water flow in spring. Sycamores have stout trunks, thick spreading branches and slender, zigzagged twigs. Their beauty is form, foliage and whitish bark that is mottled from peeling brownish flakes.

Sycamores are water-loving and in return for shading the creek they take their share. My southwestern desert sycamore canyon landscape is made up of gulches, draws and sand washes. These arteries lead away from the creek, into the benchlands and hills dressed in mesquite, catclaw, cholla, prickly pear, yucca and rabbit brush — places where Gambel's quail live.

Each time I park under the huge forest canopy next to a dark, gray, rough trunk of a sycamore tree, it brings back memories of the first time I set foot on its carpet of leaves. A stone's throw away is a glacier of washed sand that dumps into the creek. It's an easy access to the benchland overlooking the canyon.

I recall that the dogs, fresh out of the kennel boxes, flushed a large covey of Gambel's quail not far up the sandy wash. The birds flew to a grassy bench full of cholla, above the sycamores. I called the Brittanys back and scolded them for being reluctant to return, but I understood the trip to sycamore canyon had been long and I was as excited as they were. In fact I didn't even have my 20-gauge over-under out of the pickup when the birds flushed.

I do remember it didn't take long to find the scattered covey on the bench. I don't recall the number of birds the dogs pointed in the cholla patch, but my shooting certainly didn't do the dogs' performance justice. I wonder if the sycamore trees kept a tally of the number of shots that echoed through the canyon. I'm reluctant to take a partner when I hunt sycamore canyon because the sycamores have such a loveliness and loneliness that seem to demand solitude.

I was back again, parked under the same tree. Several years of sycamore leaves had floated down the stream since that first covey. The old sycamore trees hadn't changed, but I bet a lot of hunting stories have been whispered through their branches about the dogs and me. Stories about hot barrels, empty shotgun hulls and Gambel's quail.

I took out a sweet little 28-gauge Spanish Arrieta, threw the gun up to my cheek, looked down the barrels, rubbed the highly figured walnut stock and a put it back in the leather case. A few years ago I set aside my 20-gauge

I like to hunt three or four pointing dogs at a time in big open Gambel's quail country. Within the next few steps, things are about to happen for Perk Perkins.

over-under shotgun and now hunt upland game birds with a 28-gauge side by side.

Every now and then I think about my boyhood, hunting with my first shotgun, a single shot .410 gauge. With that gun the bobwhites definitely had the advantage. My next was a 12-gauge automatic I used for valley quail. That was a disaster — too big, too heavy, too slow. Then I had a 16-gauge, and a 20-gauge. Today, I'm comfortable with a 28-gauge. It's light and fast. I've come full circle, but I must say the light 16-gauge side-by -side and the 20-gauge over-under put many a quail on the ground.

With the Arrieta put away, I decided to carry the camera. My friend Jim Fergus, author of *Hunter's Road*, slipped a neat English 28-gauge double out of its case. Other than getting the dogs, we were ready. His Britt came out of the dog's compartment first, then my two dogs followed.

It was almost midday. Jim and I moved along the sandy wash, the dogs far ahead but not out of sight. At the first bifurcation, I suggested he work the draw that intersects the sandy wash. I blew the whistle several times to let the three Brittanys know that we were changing direction, as a large covey of quail flushed and came flying into the draw. The birds split into two groups. One covey landed in the draw

in a large patch of thick brush, the others kept going and settled in a cholla field on the top of a flat low hill.

"Jim," I said, "I bet the birds flushed when I called the dogs. Let's let the birds settle down a bit. I know this covey and the dogs will find them again. This draw runs parallel to the sycamore creek. The cholla ridge where part of the covey landed divides the creek and the draw. When we walk on top, you will see the pickup truck in the sycamores. Unless the birds are really pushed the only place they will fly is between the cholla ridge and the draw.

"These birds are locked in to this area and won't leave their home range. Since the birds are already broken up, I'm sure they will start calling to get together. It appears the quail in the bottom have the best cover, so I assume they will stay put longer than the bunch in the cholla.

"Let's go after the quail on top, first. I believe that covey more than likely will be running, because the cover is not as heavy. We'll walk the edge of the cholla field so we can see into the draw and also watch the top.

"If the birds flush as a unit, they will divide again. One thing I have learned, if Gambel's quail are running or flying for their own safety the birds divide, then later come back together. Let's go, you should have good shooting."

Winston, Lewis, and Mac take a break.

My two Brittanys, Mac and Hershey, and Jim's French Brittany, Henri, were on top before we got there. I was well in back of Jim, taking pictures. Two birds flushed wild almost underfoot and dove over the hill into the draw. Both birds landed in the thicket where the other group put in. I assumed the birds ran around the dogs. Far up ahead, Henri pointed, but the birds flushed wide. My two dogs off to the right of Henri were also pointing. Jim hurried past the trailing dog and three birds flushed to his right.

Jim shot and put a quail on the ground. Mac scooped it up and retrieved the bird to me. It was a fine little rooster. I figured the birds would be along the top of the edge next to the draw.

Within a minute, all three Britts locked up again and several more quail flushed and flew into the draw. I clicked off several frames with the 35mm Nixon F5 motor drive. Jim killed another bird and Henri retrievee it. Jim hurriedly slipped the bird into his vest and followed the other dogs. A single flushed, but out of range.

He stopped to water the dogs and I walked to him. "Jim, nice shooting. I believe about 10 quail have flushed so far. Do you want to cover the area again?"

"What do you think?" Jim asked.

"Well, if I were shooting I would go after the ones in the draw, the ones that just flushed. Also, I believe the birds you find in the bottom will return to the top anyway, and we can, too."

For over an hour, Jim and the dogs circled around between the draw and cholla hill. The area was 50 acres at the most, and as we suspected, the flushed birds traded back and forth between the hill and the draw, never leaving the area.

Jim killed six quail by early afternoon, and we felt the birds need to reassemble before dark. Six birds out of the sycamore covey were enough.

Driving back took an hour. Our plan was to have supper with Jim Harrison and Nick Reems. You never pass up Jim Harrison's broiled chicken with chipotle. The next day, the four of us were hunting the mesquite breaks.

Chapter Four

SCALED QUAIL

If bobwhites are kings and Gambel's are knights, then scaled quail are princes.

Oklahoma: Most members of the pheasant family (*Phasianidae*) are sought-after game birds — including all of the quail in North America. I had my first view of scaled quail near Felt, Oklahoma, when they crossed the dirt lane a mile after I turned off the blacktop.

An hour before, I sat alone at a table in a café in Boise City reading the *Atlas of Public Hunting Lands of Oklahoma* over bacon and eggs. Seated in a row at the counter were seven ranch regulars, all wearing big hats of mixed colors and high boots. If you looked only at their backs you couldn't tell the ranch hands from the ranch boss, but the dirty sweatbands and the scuffed round-heeled cowboy boots told a different story. A waitress refilled their cups, then mine, with steaming hot coffee.

Back then, small town cafes west of the Mississippi all had the same atmosphere — a counter with a row of swivel seats, a chalkboard menu, red checkered oilcloth-covered tables, patrons wearing Western or billed hats, friendly waitresses, laughter, hot coffee and all breakfasts with real hash browns.

A man wearing a big black hat seated in the center of the row motioned to the waitress, calling her by name, and with a deep laugh asked for the bill. The rest of the cowboys streamed out the door, toothpicks in their mouths.

Tom Petrie waits patiently for the two Brittanys taking a swim in a stock tank.

As he walked toward the door, the man in the black hat stopped at my table and looked down at the opened atlas and the map of Rita Blanca Wildlife Management Area, then at me.

"See you're from Montana. I buy bulls up in that country," he said. "See you have a couple birds dogs, too. Going to do a little quail hunting in these parts, ha. Better bobwhite hunting east of here."

"Sir, I've been hunting bobwhite for the past week and thought I'd try scaled quail. I've never hunted them before," I said. The big man leaned over the table, taking a pen out of his black leather vest pocket.

"Well, you are going to the right place, but blue quail are a lot different than bobwhites. They're runners, but I have never hunted them with dogs," he laughed.

My eyes followed his pen.

"From here, take Highway 56 west to Felt, go several miles, and beyond the Wildlife Management Area take that next dirt road. Drive almost to the dry creek and park by the windmill," he explained.

He made an "X" marking the windmill on the map, then a large circle and signed his name. If any one asks what you are doing when you're hunting, show them my signature. I saw blues by the water tank last week when I checked my Montana bulls." He laughed again. He moved the pen along a black line on the map, made a small dot and said, "Here is the home place. It's about 20 miles down this road. If you have time after hunting, stop by and let me know how the dogs did. Never ran dogs on blues," he said.

"I plan to hunt a couple of days. Would it be all right if I hunt your place tomorrow, too?"

"Man after my own heart," he said. "Help yourself."

The waitress appeared and offered me more hot coffee. He put the pen back in one pocket and from the other well-worn pocket took out a can of snooze. The big man tapped the can's cover several times and said, "Sally, this young man may be coffee-ed out. I believe he is ready to go bird hunting." He opened the snooze can, took a scoop with his thumb, and laughed before putting the chew in his mouth.

I thanked the man in the big hat as he turned away and walked out the door. Then I thanked the waitress, but refused the coffee, and asked for the bill. Four strips of bacon, two bright yellow eggs, homemade toast, a large side of hash browns, and all the coffee I could drink cost two dollars and 50 cents, plus the tip. I wouldn't need lunch.

My two Brittanys, Shoe and Daisy, raced for the water

tank straight out of the kennel boxes. I walked towards the windmill, its twirling shadow highlighting numerous quail tracks on the ground. The dogs jumped out of the tank, their bellies dripping, and shook water 10 feet in all directions on the dry sand.

Several white-crested bluish-gray birds dashed away in a blur of running feet. Then suddenly, two gray streaks burst from my right, twisted through the high rabbit brush, and flew over a low grassy hill. Both Brittanys began to work vigorously, then suddenly pointed. At least 20 quail flushed and followed the other two birds over the hill. Still others ran up the hill in the direction of the flushed birds. Daisy broke and dashed through the running birds, scattering them over the hill.

I carefully worked diagonally across the hill to the top of the ridge and looked into a shallow basin of short grass and low shrubs. A mesquite-lined sandy wash ran through the basin. On this cloudless warm day the wind felt stronger walking the ridge. Looking back the windmill was still moving at a slow pace. I stopped to let the light breeze cool my face. The dogs came alongside and I sat between them, looking into the basin.

I thought about how many times I had lived this moment bird hunting? The basin's short grass and scattered shrubs reminded me of Montana. The golden grass rolled like the Northern prairies of home. It was enough to know that scaled quail run and that I have never experienced scaled quail hunting before. I had no idea what to expect. But, just like hunting gray partridge, the covey had vanished.

Before I went, the dogs seemed to sense the country had birds. By the time I reloaded the Browning 20-gauge superimposed shotgun, the Brittanys were halfway to the sandy wash. I walked the grassy flat on one side of the wash for another half hour, but failed to find any birds. I made a pass on the other side of the wash for several hundred yards and saw no tracks. I called Shoe and Daisy, gave them a drink and rubbed a handful of cool water across each dog's back. I took a long drink and put the canteen back in my vest.

The dogs, a little wet and refreshed, headed for a terrace below the low ridge. Scattered mesquite, prickly pear, junipers and other short shrubs encroached the semi-arid landform. I wondered aloud, if Huns like mixed shrub-grassland places, so should scaled quail. Then I realized the low ridge divided the terrace and windmill by less than 300 yards. I visualized the main covey of quail.

Most had flown over the top of the ridge, hooked a hard right and landed in the flat terrace. I had walked much too far down the slope and too far to the right of where the birds had flown over the top.

I passed several clumps of mesquite. The two dogs, not far ahead, walked gingerly to avoid the tall prickly pear. Even though the vegetation was different, I hunted a place back home so similar it was eerie. I don't recall much about that day, other than Huns seemed to be everywhere. Here, I felt the presence of quail.

I walked under the next tree, a tall magnificent mesquite. Curled bean-like pods without seeds lay beneath the crooked branches. In open patches of sandy soil, countless quail tracks lead in the direction the dogs and I were traveling.

We moved into the wind, the dogs alert, quartering to each side of the grassy strip. Every open patch of ground had quail tracks, but the space between footprints was widening. "Running quail," I said aloud, and quickened my pace.

Inside a minute, the dogs were at the end of the grassy strip standing motionless, peering into a large area of unfriendly cacti. As I approached the cactus, the dogs charged. At the end of the thick cover, certainly 40 feet away, the covey came up. Four, six, 10 and then a big wave of two to three dozen birds flushed and scattered, flying over the top of the ridge towards the windmill.

The dogs had not come out of the cactus patch, so I skirted around the edge. Then they were 10 feet in front of me. I was not ready as two birds flushed underfoot. I missed the first shot, being too much in a hurry, shooting in back of the lead bird, then relaxed and killed the trailing quail with the second barrel. It fell almost on Shoe's head. He scooped up the bird and retrieved it to me. Not a feather on the bird was ruffled. I held my first scaled quail, turning it over and over in my hands.

Several more birds flushed, but still admiring the bird's beautiful markings, I forgot to reload the shotgun and I didn't even watch the last birds fly off. One would think after all the years of hunting upland game birds I would not get buck fever, but then again it was my first scalie. As I walked back to the pickup, I realized there was a lot that I didn't know about hunting scaled quail.

Approximate range of the scaled quail.

KNOWING THE BIRD

Scaled Quail Origins: The scaled quail (*Callipepla squamata*) has two subspecies. It's an attractive game bird and the second most hunted in the Southwest. In southern Arizona, the subspecies is called the Arizona scaled quail (*C. s. pallida*) and it is better known because the bird has the largest range. The Arizona scaled quail has a buff-colored belly. The other subspecies is the chestnut-bellied scaled quail (*C. s. castanagastris*) and its range is limited to south Texas and parts of Mexico.

Attempts to transplant the scaled quail to other regions have generally failed. There is evidence of successful transplantation in Colorado, where the birds did spread and expand their original range. But present distribution and the historical range of the scaled quail have changed little. Scaled quail and Gambel's quail share a large area in Arizona and New Mexico. Even though they are in the same geographic area, the two species use different elevations and habitat within that range.

In most of their range, scaled quail are referred to as "scalie." The name comes from the distinctive scalloping on the breast, nape of the neck, and belly. In some places the bird is called "cottontop" because both sexes display a white fluffy crest, much like pulled cotton. In Texas and Oklahoma they are called "blue quail" because their plumage has an overall bluish-gray tint.

DISTRIBUTION

The scaled quail is native to the arid sections of southeastern Arizona, most of New Mexico, southeastern Colorado, western and southern Texas and northern Mexico. Most of the scaled quail's distribution is in the Chihuahuan Desert and the adjacent desert grassland savanna. The geographical ranges of the scaled quail are largely unoccupied by other quail, except where the Gambel's quail range overlaps in the bordering states of Arizona and New Mexico.

I have spent a great deal of time hunting in the areas shared by both species, even though I look for each species in a different landscape. The Gambel's quail lives in the lower dry habitat and brushy washes, whereas the scalies reside in the grassy draws, hillsides and plateaus above the dense desert habitat. If one is only after scaled quail, western Texas is a good bet. In Oklahoma, the best scaled quail hunting is in Cimarron County, although the bird does occur in other counties as well.

IN THE BUSH, IN THE HAND

A scaled quail is a magnificent specimen in the hand, although its colors are not as striking as other members of the quail family. If one looks closely, the bird is not plainly clad. Each feather has a finely barred or scaled pattern that has an iridescent silky glow. The colors are soft, with a rich mix of blues and sliver grays — not the grays of fighting soldiers, but the stately sliver-grays of a noble prince. To me the scaled quail is prince of the game birds.

The scaled quail is larger than Gambel's quail. Adult males average a little over 7 ounces, whereas a male Gambel's quail will average only 6 ounces. The adult male is about 11 inches long and has a wingspan of 13 to 14 inches. He also has a uniform pearly gray unstreaked throat and a white fluffy crest, like pulled cotton.

Unlike other quail, both the male and female scaled quail appear similar, but upon close examination a rooster's uniform appears more scaly than the hen's. Females are drabber in color and not as princely. The hen also has light

Scaled quail, sometimes called "cottontops," blend well with their surroundings.

brown streaks on the sides of the face and throat and her cottontop is buff colored and less conspicuous.

The two subspecies of scaled quail that live in the United States have different color phases due to the dissimilar habitat areas, but these colors variations of pale sliver gray to pale grayish blue are similar. Young birds are practically indistinguishable from adults after the first winter, except for their outer primary wing feathers.

Scaled quail frequently communicate with one another and many times you can hear the birds before they spot you. Listen for the soft *churrs churrs churrs* sound. When scaled quail become scattered they use an assembly call and are very vocal, but like other quail, they do not start calling immediately. Give them time and listen for their two-syllable call *chip-churr, chip-churr, chip-churr.* The scaled quail's assembly call is easy to pinpoint on the ground.

LIFE CYCLE AND BEHAVIOR

Scaled quail form large coveys that remain together during the winter and begin to break up before March. Birds are sexually mature their first year and courtship starts after breakup of the covey. The males call from a mesquite tree or some other high perch. Like Gambel's quail, the male displays by strutting and chasing before the female. The male does not defend an area so a territory is really not established. Males do challenge other males, but real combat is rare.

Although the scaled quail starts to mate in April, their brooding period can be delayed because of lack of rain. Scaled quail continue their pair bond throughout the summer and if seasonal rains are late, the hen will delay her nesting activity. When rains do come, green vegetation becomes abundant, the birds feed, and the green vegetation directly stimulates hormones related to successful reproduction.

The scaled quail hen makes a simple scraped-out nest on the ground and lines it with grass and a few feathers. The male helps in the nest building activity. Her nest is built in fairly open grassy country and usually has some type of brushy cactus canopy overhead. The average clutch is 10 to 14 eggs and incubation takes about 21 days. The success of the hatch determines the number of birds going into the fall.

The male stays near the nest during incubation and is alert for danger to the hen. If the first nest is lost, the hen may re-nest if conditions are favorable. Many times a male will take over the duties of the female if she is killed.

If scaled quail do delay nesting due to seasonal weather conditions, or if a hen re-nests, young of different ages can be seen at the same time of year. Scaled quail can have hatches coming off as late as October, but this does not mean a hen has brought off two broods in one season. Studies have shown no evidence of scaled quail having a double clutch.

When the last chick has hatched, both parents lead the chicks from the nest. Chicks are vigorous and can follow the adults as soon as their down is dry. Day-old chicks can already run. The chicks' main diet is animal matter of many kinds. Both adults use calls to communicate with their young and lead them to good feed areas. The calls also keep the chicks together. If danger approaches, the mother calls and the chicks immediately disappear. Young birds start to make short flights within a week. The chicks' activity and mobility develops rapidly, and within two weeks the young birds can fly.

As long as the young birds need attention, the brood stays together, which can last until early fall. But as the juveniles mature, their bonds with adults weaken. By late fall multiple families and stray singles have joined together and maternal instincts diminish.

The scaled quail is unquestionably a terrestrial bird. It has strong legs that it uses to its advantage in the open country. The bird prefers to escape by running rather than flying. But scaled quail will fly if pushed or surprised. Their flight is longer than Gambel's quail and once they're back on the ground, birds will run to better cover.

HABITAT

The scaled quail is a familiar game bird in the semiarid desert, essentially the grassy uplands with less brushy areas. They also use mesquite savannah country — endless grass-covered plains with scattered trees. Their desert grasslands generally are between 2,500 to 5,000 feet in elevation and are connected by or interspersed with rugged arroyos, steep canyons and thorny forests full of unfriendly plants. Some of the savannah country's backdrop is outlined with dark evergreen oak mountains and cobalt blue skies, a place where it feels as if most of the air has never been used and the wind is a descendant of the grasses.

Unlike the Gambel's quail, the vegetation in which the scaled quail prefers to live is mixed shrubs, but open and sometimes even spare grass cover. That is why they are notorious runners and would rather not fly to escape their enemies. This Western quail evades dense thickets, tall brush and tree-lined washes. The scaled quail lives in a landscape of mesas, rolling hills, low ridges, wide draws and open grassy cover. Even though there can be steep slopes and rugged terrain within this landscape, scaled quail are not particularly attached to those types of landforms. Where these two different habitats come together, scaled quail and Gambel's quail overlap. When trees and scrubby plants overtake grasslands, scaled quail populations disappear, but if shrubs are completely cleared this also has an effect on the population.

Some areas of creosote bush association and irrigated lands are also used by scaled quail. The birds are quick to take advantage of feed or water around ranches and farmsteads since the necessities of life are never overabundant in the desert.

Like all desert creatures, the scaled quail is rarely seen when the sun is high overhead. One of my favorite areas to hunt has a dry creek running through it. Both sides of the wide arroyo are lined with mesquite, hackberry, catclaw, beargrass, cholla, prickly pear and many other unfriendly cacti. On each side, beyond the heavy tangle of cover that follows the creek, are perennial grasslands, intermixed covers, some burroweed soapweed yucca and mesquite. Along the creek every mile or so is a manmade reservoir with an earthen dam at one end. In the southwest these are called "tanks." Grass and mixed forbs grow around each tank to the highwater mark.

Small flocks of blue-winged teal or shovelers are usually at home on the tank when I arrive, but are the first to leave when I step out of the pickup. A killdeer or a sandpiper is usually next, but they fly only to the other side of the pond. The ducks always make two or three wide swings around the reservoir before they go to another tank. Life centers around those tanks. Bird and animal tracks are imprinted in the soft soil at the edge of the water.

Sometimes when I get out of the hunting rig I flush a covey of Gambel's or scalies. Other times the quail will run to their cover. I can tell which species runs or flushes, not only by identifying the birds, but by noting the direction the quail go to their different habitat types. The Gambel's quail highways all go to the brushy wide arroyo while the scaled quail trails lead to the cholla grasslands.

Seth Hadley and Ben Brown relax with their Brittanys
before hunting scaled quail in the vast semi-arid savannah country.

FOOD AND WATER

About 30 percent of the adult scaled quail diet is animal matter, which is a higher percentage than other quail. The other 70 percent is vegetable matter. Young birds feed almost exclusively on animal matter. As the young birds grow, their food selection changes to greens.

The birds' habitat is home to a large number of beetles, grasshoppers, ants, spiders, weevils and other insects upon which the scaled quail feed. There is a large carrying capacity for animal life in the desert grasslands and the sandy soil has many open patches without ground cover, making it easy for young and adult quail to feed on insects and other invertebrates.

In summer and fall, scaled quail feed on fruits, flowers, leaves and seeds as these foods become available. Of the vegetable matter consumed by scaled quail, most is in the form of seeds and fruits. Even though scaled quail live in the desert grasslands, few grasses are eaten. The grasslands do have many forbs, and weed seeds are eaten in large amounts. Among the birds' favorite foods are pigweed Russian thistle, gumweed, bindweed, catclaw, mustard, lupine and mesquite, to name a few.

As winter approaches, scaled quail move to the foothills where they feed on a wide variety of shrubs and forbs. In late winter and early spring, greens become available, which triggers the spring breakup and pairing.

Scaled quail are better adapted to heat and require less water than other quail. Water requirements are largely met by consuming foods that have lots of moisture, but other factors play an important part in the birds' reduced water requirements. One is they consume more insects than other quail. Also, the birds feed on many succulent fruits like prickly pear and other cacti.

Although water is not essential, except during long periods of drought, birds will gather around open water, but do not necessarily use it every day. Scaled quail also travel greater distances than Gambel's quail for water and succulent plants.

Along the dry creek, the one with all the quail highways and the earthen dam, I find scaled quail trails leading a lot farther away from the reservoir than the Gambel's quail trails. And when hunting around this tank, I find scaled quail can be in a much larger radius from the open water than Gambel's quail. Windmills and water tanks are better indicators for finding Gambel's than for scalies.

DAILY ROUTINE

Daily activities for scaled quail start at dawn. They often begin feeding at daybreak along a hillside or ridge. After feeding for a couple of hours, the covey may travel to water, but this does not occur every day and most watering takes place mid-morning.

Early morning and late afternoon are the most active times of the day for the birds. By midday, the desert grasslands heat up and almost every living creature slows down. During the heat of the day, quail seek shade and spend time resting, loafing and taking dust baths in the loose sand. Roosting areas do change every night, but they can be in the same vicinity.

In late winter, the scaled quail's range shrinks in size. You may think of a quail's range as circle, but more often than not it's an elongated space. This irregular shape follows the best food, water, resting and roosting cover. Seldom is the home range longer than a mile. The exception is that in dry years the birds' range can expand. In spring, this home range becomes larger and by late summer larger still. Daily travel in summer varies. Although the birds' range is large and can cover several miles, this does not mean scaled quail will travel this distance in one day.

There is a mesa not far from the mountains and a canyon with an underground stream that supplies water to a flat, grassy plain. The underground water follows an arroyo and is marked by scattered rows of sycamores and mesquite. This is a haunt of not only scaled quail, but once was occupied by outlaws. These outlaws are now in history, but the scaled quail still remain in good numbers.

I drive along over a winding trail, dodging thorny shrubs and clumps of cactus. Other than me, only a few ranch hands and cowboys use the sandy trail.

I'm never surprised when I see the covey of scalies, for this is the home covey and they live within 20 acres of the adobe. At first they are almost invisible, dressed in their silver-gray uniforms that match the surroundings. The birds do not attempt to fly, but scurry down the sandy lane with remarkable speed, their heads high and white cottontops erect. Sometimes they run in single file, other times zig-zagging in and out among the desert cover. The scaled quail are soon out of sight, but reappear again crossing a sandy opening far ahead.

I call them the adobe covey. Sometimes I see them in the yard chasing grasshoppers. Sometimes I see them in the garden gleaning insect from the vegetables. But most of the time I see them along the loose, sandy lane.

When I park under the large sycamore not far from the adobe, I tell my hunting guest not to walk in the direction of the home covey. I have learned a lot about the daily activities of scaled quail from the home adobe covey.

HUNTING SCALED QUAIL THEN

From the book *Game Birds of North America,* by Daniel Giraud Elliot. London, Suckling & Co. 1897. An excerpt, page 50:

A dog is practically useless for hunting the Scaled Partridge, for if he is well broken and attempts to point a covey, the birds will run several hundred yards while he is standing, and then will add several hundred more, while he is trailing them, and the poor animal becomes bewildered and disgusted and is apt to run also. I know nothing so trying to the patience of a sportsman as the tactics of this species, unless it be the similar habits of other Crested Quail.

From the book *Life Histories of North American Gallinaceous Birds,* by Arthur Cleveland Bent. United States National Museum, Bulletin 162. Smithsonian Institution, Washington D. C. U.S. Government Printing Office Washington. 1932. An excerpt, page 57:

Game hunting the blue quail will never figure as one of the major sports, although it is a gamy bird and makes a delicious and plump morsel for the table. The birds are widely scattered over a vast expanse of rough country, on desert plains covered with thorny underbrush, or on stony or rocky foothills where walking is difficult and slow. The hunter must be prepared to do some long, hard tramping, for he is more likely to count the number of miles to a bird than the number of birds to a mile. A dog is useless, for these quail have not yet acquired the habit of lying to a dog. Eastern quail have learned to lie close, a good way to hide from human enemies but a very poor way to escape from the many predatory animal enemies in the West. Scaled quail are shier than Gambel's quail and are generally first seen in the distance running rapidly and dodging around among the bushes. They run faster than man can walk and the hunter must make fast progress over the rough ground to catch up with them. By the time he gets within range he will be nearly out of breath and will have to take a quick snap shot at the fleeting glimpse of a small gray bird dodging between bushes. This is far more difficult, under the circumstances, than wing shooting and can not be considered pot shooting. Sometimes, when a large covey has been scattered and rattled, the hunter may surprise single birds and get an occasional wing shot: but they are apt to jump from most unexpected places, ahead of or behind the hunter, and give him a difficult shot. Late in the season they are often found in large packs of 100 or 200 birds, when the chances for good sport are better. Even then the hunter may well feel proud of a hard-earned bag.

HUNTING SCALED QUAIL TODAY

If I hunt early in the day, I work the ridges for scaled quail first. That is where they are going to be feeding. Then I walk the low hillsides, sometimes not far below the ridges. Scaled quail seem to like to have a view of their surroundings. I make sure I cover the mesquite and other brushy patches on the hillsides.

Dogs have to learn the ways of scaled quail. Like hunting the big, open, Northern prairie grasslands for gray partridge and sharp-tailed grouse, open semi-desert grassland is a place for big running dogs. I hunt scaled quail about the same way I do gray partridge, by putting three or four dogs down at a time. For every mile a man walks, a dog will run 10 miles. Scalie country is big and to find a covey, dogs need to cover lots of ground. When hunting savannah habitat, it's possible to see dogs at a great distance, so trust your dogs and let them push out to several hundred yards.

My dogs point running birds, then relocate several times after I arrive, and we will eventually break up the covey. When a covey starts to run, the birds break up into smaller and smaller groups. As with all species of quail when pursued, the covey splits into smaller numbers for the survival of the group, then regroups when danger has passed. Some will flush ahead of the dog, but many will hold tight. Walk slowly, circling the area, and let the dog work the scattered singles and small groups.

I've had great luck hunting scalies with pointing dogs. While scaled quail can be difficult for some dogs, I believe it's just a matter of the dog adjusting to a new species of game bird. After several outings hunting scaled quail in savannah country, one learns several important things:

One: Scaled quail congregate in large coveys, numbering as many as 60 or more birds. Once the birds are aware of you and the dogs, walk slowly after them. The large covey will break up when followed, but walk leisurely, giving the birds time to scatter in all directions.

Two: Some birds will flush, some will fan out holding tight, and others will run circling in back of the dog and hunter. For the birds that flush, keep a careful eye on their direction of flight. Before going after the birds that have flown, give them time to disperse some scent. Hunt the quail that are still on the ground by walking a wide circle. Once the covey is scattered, singles and small groups of birds hold extremely tight.

Three: Cover the area where you think the covey put down thoroughly. At times some of the birds will run on landing and head for heavy tufts of grass and hide. Be persistent and walk, hunting an enlarged circle from where you think the birds put in.

Four: Hunt the scattered birds slowly, working the dogs fairly close. Once a bird or two is found the rest will be close by, even though many may run. Scaled quail singles in good cover set tight for a dog. Once flushed, a scalie is a strong flyer and goes farther than other quail because of the open country.

Five: Cover the area over and over again. The quail are there and it's just a matter of being patient. Once hidden, single scaled quail do not like to fly. After several minutes birds will start calling. Calling birds are usually on the move looking to join other singles and to reassemble as soon as possible, even though this can take more than an hour.

To me, hunting scaled quail is more like hunting Huns than other quail. They are a bird of the prairie and I find them a real challenge for me and the dogs.

BIRD OF THE SAVANNAH

Most of my hunting adventures for scaled quail are in Arizona and New Mexico. When many hunters think of hunting the Southwest, they visualize sandy arroyos, mesquite, cactus, roadrunners and rattlesnakes. It always comes as a surprise when they discover that grasslands also exist there, even though these grasslands are not like Eastern meadows or Northern plains.

Hunting scaled quail is different than hunting Gambel's or Mearns' quail, even though all three species may be in the same vicinity. Because the birds live in this open landscape and their cruising range is larger, scaled quail are not nearly as predictable as their desert cousins. The scaled quail's movements are like a soft desert grassland breeze — one day they're all around you, the next day they're gone.

Late one afternoon, a couple of winters ago, long after my first encounter with scaled quail in Oklahoma and with a lot more experience hunting scalies, I hunted with a

landowner who had lived in the Southwest most of his adult life. Drum Hadley was a knowledgeable Western quail hunter and knew where the scaled quail hung out. The temperature was over 85 degrees, and like most desert creatures, the scaled quail is rarely out in the bright hot sun.

We turned off the main gravel road onto a dirt lane that wandered through a series of grassy draws and stopped by a old windmill. The ancient machine was singing a see-saw tune when I stepped out of the pickup to water the dogs. Below the rusty iron skyscraper, a long steel pipe spewed out precious, crystal clear water from a deep concrete stock tank. The dogs took advantage of it.

Nothing moved except the wind pushing against the blades of the windmill. The only sound was the grinding of the gears, the water spilling in the tank and the dogs splashing water. I walked toward an old adobe foundation lived in years ago by the first residents that used this clear water.

Suddenly, the sky darkened and the windmill stopped, then spun around 180 degrees and the blades became a blur. A stiff wind came up strong as lightning flashed. Drum and I put the dogs back up and hopped into the pickup as torrential rain blocked much of our view through the windshield. As the rain fell, the tank filled and a puddle of water became a small lake. Then the rain stopped as quickly as it started.

I rolled down the truck window and was about to get out when a flock of scaled quail materialized on the grassy, gently sloping hillside above the pickup. When I stepped out of the hunting rig the large covey ran over the top of the hill and out of sight. It looked to me like there were more than 60 birds.

A slight breeze funneled down the draw, carrying the sweet smell of the desert after a rain. All three dogs where pointing in the direction I saw the quail disappear. Drum and I pulled the dogs from the fresh scent and headed down the main draw. We walked about 400 yards before turning uphill, circling the large covey of birds and hunting them into the wind.

After 20 minutes, the three dogs locked up on point. Drum and I pushed hard; we could see the birds running ahead. The dogs kept pointing as we went and finally with a roar of the wings the big covey scattered, flew and settled down several hundred yards away across a large, open, grassy flat.

III

Seth Hadley's two Brittanys work a scattered covey of "scalies" in the ideal habitat.

Scaled quail hunting is rarely that easy, but after a good hard rain, scenting conditions change for the better. The dogs made a number of great points on singles and even a few on doubles. Together we killed half a dozen birds, enough for the dogs to make some good retrieves. We returned to the windmill and cleaned the birds in the cool water the windmill pumped from under the sandy desert ground.

Combination hunts for scaled quail, Gambel's quail and Mearns' are ideal, as all three species can be in the same general area. The important thing to remember is the type of habitat each bird requires.

GUNNING IN THE WIND

From Alaska to Mexico, the wind swings down the eastern slope of the Rocky Mountain Front, bending the Midwest sea of grass, before sweeping thousands of miles to the forests of eastern North America. On the western edge of the prairie, the wind bows the junipers that creep down from the mountain foothills to meet the plains. The wind travels across the intermountain shrub grasslands, the shortgrass prairie, the mixed prairie, and the tallgrass prairie. It moves the lonely windmills and prairie pumps,

supplying precious water for thirsty cattle. Windmills, the ones that still remain, are prairie monuments to folks that stayed.

The wind moves the evergreen oaks, the cholla, the yucca, and funnels through the mesquite-lined creek beds and sand washes of the high desert. It ripples the ponds, the lakes, the reservoirs, and breaths life into the wildfires that in turn give new life to the savannas.

Wind drives prairie snows leaving a mosaic of white and gold — a patchwork on the landscape and open feeding places for creatures large and small. Wind, rain, cold, heat and drought influence all living things, including man.

For the Western bird hunter, wind is part of the hunting experience and certainly plays a role in wingshooting on the open prairies and savannas.

Wind also plays an important part in game birds' survival and behavior. It rearranges the landscapes, removing soil, sending seeds on their way and redistributing water to other places. I think of the prairie as earth's mixing bowl and the wind as the spoon.

A light wind makes for fine wingshooting, but a strong wind can bring one's shooting score down. In morning, a light wind seems like magic, carrying the dew along with it.

The author's dog Winston makes a fine retrieve for his master.

Midday, when the sun is high, a strong breeze is ideal for a pointing dog scenting birds. Most evenings, the wind subsides and takes on a softness, transforming the prairie into a world of stillness.

The dry mesquite savanna country west of the southern Rocky Mountain Front needed moisture. It hadn't rained for more than forty days, but the five-day forecast called for change. A low pressure system from the West Coast was moving in, bringing with it high winds. The weather map showed the major system moving northwest.

I'd been here a week. My hunting partner, Steve Smith, was to arrive early evening and we planned to spent the next three days hunting quail. With only three days, I felt we had to cram as much quail hunting in as possible. I was encouraged by the weather forecast.

The quail population had been high, but due to the hot, dry weather the dogs' performance was only average. Coveys they could find, but singles were almost impossible to locate. Dry soil and the lack of humidity are the main reasons dogs have difficulty scenting birds. Add a little moisture, plus some wind, and the whole picture changes. A large covey of desert quail will seldom hold for a dog, but singles do. So when hunting these swift little desert rockets,

finding singles is the name of the game.

The next morning, the weather was changing rapidly and looked promising. The eastern horizon was ablaze in orange, sending long rays of sunlight toward the overcast western sky. A large frontal system was moving eastward, its moist black belly crawling over the high mountains. The temperature, in the low 60s, was dropping before a cool moist breeze.

Lunch fixins, dogs and gear loaded, Steve and I headed out for a full day of quail hunting. Seth Hadley, with his hunting partner Rick Ruoff, followed us in his hunting rig. The place Seth and I had planned to hunt first was about an hour's drive from the ranch. Here the big open savanna country with grassy, rolling hills and a wide dry wash lined with mesquite was a great place for both scaled and Gambel's quail.

By the time we rolled to a stop, the wind had picked up, changed direction, and was now coming out of the southwest. As I stepped from the pickup, my hat went flying off my head and it clung to a tall rabbit bush twisting in the wind 20 yards away. I went to retrieve the hat, but it kept jumping from bush to bush. Finally, I managed to snag it after four or five attempts.

When I returned to the pickup, Steve was holding his 20-gauge side-by-side shotgun under his right arm, breach open. His left hand was pushing an orange hat on his head. The wind whipping up through the empty barrels made a low whistling sound. Steve wore a half smile; the smile of a ruffed-grouse and woodcock hunter who is used to the protection of the heavy woods.

"Steve," I said, "there's a slight breeze picking up."

Still holding on to his hat, Steve responded, "Ya, it's an outright gale where I come from."

Seth put two Brittanys on the ground and I did the same. We decided to hunt the dry wash first and work the long sloping leeward hillside on the way back. I figured the birds would be either in the dry creek bottom or on the lee side below the ridge, out of the strong wind.

The warm, dry wind pushed across the wash, and it wasn't long before Seth's dog, Winston, pointed a large covey of Gambel's quail. The birds flushed from the high rabbit brush, out of gun range. The wind caught their wings and the covey scattered, a few quail screaming past us. Both Seth and Steve killed an incoming bird. I was touting a camera and missed a good photo opportunity. Rick didn't shoot, but Rick never shoots much. He's happy if he only kills one bird a day. Most of the birds flew low over the rabbit brush, under the wind and ahead of us.

Once the birds had scattered, we worked the next 200 yards slowly, encouraging the pointing dogs to work the high cover several times. The singles were almost impossible to find, but we did manage to kill a few more birds.

We walked several hundred yards following the dry wash before turning back. The wind had increased throughout the morning. Even on the hillside, it was kicking up sand and bending the golden dry grass to its roots. There I found a couple of small bunches of scaled quail, a covey apparently broken up by a red-tailed hawk, as the large majestic bird was perched high on a rock outcropping, watching and fighting the wind as we were.

At the top of the hill, Seth could not locate his dogs and separated from us to look for them. Like my dogs, if his Winston or Jasper are gone for some time, they're usually pointing birds. Steve, Rick, and I sat on the ground leaning against the pickup out of the wind.

It's not unusual for a large covey of scaled quail to flush upon seeing a hunter, but the dogs will find them glued to the golden grass the other side of the draw.

We were all but finished with lunch when Winston and Jasper joined us, with Seth not far behind, all smiles. He found the dogs pointing and on the way back, moved four coveys of scaled quail. I made no comment, but thought about the wind. Was it a hunter's curse or a blessing? After lunch, we decided not to pursue the four coveys, but try for Mearns' quail instead. Mearns' prefer rocky coulees and evergreen oaks, those kind of places protected from turbulent winds.

Many hunters hesitate to hunt when it's windy, but I don't! More than anything a hunter has to have confidence in his pointing dog while hunting in heavy wind. The biggest disadvantage for the dog in high-wind conditions is that the scent is almost always moving close to the ground. If given the opportunity, dogs will adapt quite well. I have found that a hard wind bends the grass, locks in the bird scent and sometimes helps the dogs find birds at great distances.

When hunting prairie game birds I have a mental scale for reading the wind: (1) A light air movement, five to 10 miles per hour, cools my face, moves seed pods slowly and helps dogs find birds. (2) A strong breeze of 15 but less than 20 miles per hour makes the golden quaky leaves shiver along the draws and is ideal for pointing dogs. (3) If the wind is in the 30s pushing the tumbleweeds across the open fields, the dog can pick up bird scent a long way off. (4) At 40, it's still good hunting and the dogs seem to love running the open wind, using their noses in ways unknown to us. (5) Fifty and 60 mph is still all right for pointing dogs and does not turn me back, for then I hunt the leeward draws and creek bottoms. (6) Above 70, the wind has a different sound. It makes the grass whistle, it roars down the slopes and rumbles in my ears. It is evident everywhere on the prairie and some days the dogs and I turn back.

To me, the wind is exciting with smells of distance in it. Crossing a cholla desert or an unbroken sage flat, wind gives even our pitiful sense of smell meaning. Wind blows my hair, rearranges my hat, moistens my eyes leaving teardrops on my shooting glasses. Any wind in my face is far better than four closed-in walls.

Chapter Five

MEARNS' QUAIL

Mearns' quail, once called harlequin quail, may look like comical actors,
but they can make a clown out of you.

Montana: That evening so many years ago when Jeff and I studied the Coronado National Forest maps spread across my kitchen table, my thoughts were focused on Mearns' quail. Our plans were to hunt Gambel's quail in his home state of Arizona after he graduated from Montana State University. He knew where the Gambel's quail hung out, but nothing of evergreen oak quail. This would be a good opportunity to collect my last two species of North American quail. I figured Gambel's quail should be easy but knew little about Mearns' quail.

I accomplished phase one of my plan—Gambel's quail—the first day I hunted with Jeff. After the first day,

Jeff and I hunted Gambel's four more days and had good results. On the next phase, I thought I would have to strike out on my own to find Mearns' quail country until Jeff made a phone call.

That Monday in Wilcox, population under 2,500, an elderly man wearing a worn green Forest Service cap asked if I was Jeff's friend when I walked up to his table in a local cafe. I identified him by his green cap; he recognized me by a fistful of National Forest maps. We shook hands. I placed the maps on the table and the waitress filled my coffee cup. John had spent his entire career working in the Coronado National Forest as a Forest Service employee.

"Ben, I've been retired for quite some time, but I'll show you a few places I find quail," he said. John opened a map and made several folds before placing it on the table. He took a pen from his shirt pocket and started making circles in different areas on the map. "There," he said, "that should get you started. Jeff said he hunted with you in Montana and recommended you highly. I've been saving these places for my son in the Air Force, so when he's home we have a good place to hunt.

"The Coronado National Forest is broken up into many large parcels. It's all public land and once you get into the shrub grassland with the oaks, the chance of finding Mearns' quail is good. It's also possible to find Gambel's and scaled quail in the same general area. For the past several years I haven't hunted much, but when I did, more than once I got an Arizona Grand Slam. That's all three species of quail in one day."

John wanted to see my two Brittanys when breakfast was finished.

"So, this is Shoe and McGillie," he said. "Jeff told me he had a great time hunting with you and your dogs. If my son is home sometime when you're here, would it be all right for us to go along?"

"You are welcome anytime," I said. I thanked him; we shook hands and exchanged address cards.

I drove, looking more at the map than the road. I noticed the elevation had changed since leaving Wilcox. I had left the desert floor, climbing, following the contours of rugged foothills towards the mountains. The topography was a series of rocky canyons within an oak savanna. Blankets of golden bunchgrasses and scattered evergreen oaks covered the hillsides. Beyond the hills, the mountains appeared as a painter's palette. Colors of Hooker's and emerald green, golden ocher, burnt sienna, burnt umber, Payne's gray and cobalt blue were emphasized by the bright sun.

I passed the turnoff, backed up, checked the map again to see if it was the right road, then made a sharp turn onto a narrow, rocky lane. Most of the roads in this country were nothing but fist-sized crushed rock, but I felt secure with my four-wheel drive. I put the pickup in low and crawled down the steep incline. The mud-and-snow tires gripped the rocky trail for several hundred yards. I stopped at trail's end next to a tree-lined, sandy arroyo and parked the pickup between two large emery oaks. It seemed this was the only flat place in the canyon and had just enough space to back the hunting rig around.

I checked the map again to make sure I was parked in the right place. John had drawn three circles marked "quail" and an "X" indicating where to park. Two marks were down the wash and the other one was in the next draw that ran parallel to the tree-lined arroyo.

It was mid-January and the sun shined on the western slope of the canyon, and at this time of day, it also shined almost down to the wash. By noon, the day would be hot—in the 80s. It hadn't rained since I'd been there, which is not unusual for southern Arizona that time of year. My first thought was water because the weather and the terrain were going to be tough on the dogs.

Shoe and McGillie were on the ground running the wash while I loaded my vest with 20-gauge shells, a large canteen of water, a ham sandwich and an apple. Around my neck hung a whistle, compass and forceps. The over-under Belgium Browning shotgun came out last. I whistled the two dogs back and they returned with their bellies dripping water.

The water came as a surprise. I followed the wet trail in the sand into the arroyo and walked the tree-lined wash, the dogs running out in front. Within 20 yards both dogs were lying in a clear, deep pool of water beneath an overhanging rock cliff. Several smaller disconnected pools followed the sandy arroyo that lead toward the Hooker's green mountains. At each pool I stopped and looked around the perimeter for quail tracks, bird scratching and feathers, but found nothing.

Within three hours we had worked both sides of the arroyo from the lowest to the highest elevation in the canyon. It was hot and the dogs kept returning to the cool pools. I wondered occasionally if my scant knowledge of the species was the reason I wasn't finding any birds. Or was it that I wasn't covering the right habitat that time of day. Or was it that the dogs couldn't pick up scent in the hot, dry weather. Maybe it was all three, yet I realized just walking in the right place could change things.

The dogs and I had been at it for a long time with no evidence of quail. I had thoroughly covered both areas in the arroyo marked on the map. Late afternoon kind of crept up on me; the sun was now shining on the opposite side of the canyon. I could feel the time of year, sort of like winter sliding down the evergreen mountains.

Evergreen oaks — that's what came to mind hunting this mystery bird. I was looking through one of them at the

*Seth Hadley hunts this typical Mearn's quail habitat of rolling hills,
deep canyons filled with evergreen oaks and manzanita.*

low sun. Shadows danced in front of my lug-soled boots. Both dogs returned, each sitting alongside me and pressing their noses against the plastic wrap of the ham sandwich. I split the sandwich three ways and ate the apple myself.

I was left wondering if I should hunt the last circled place. According to the map, the draw that paralleled this arroyo was a half-mile walk from the pickup. Or should I hunt in some other area circled on the map.

I made a decision. The dogs and I climbed out of the canyon and walked toward the draw. For an hour there was no sign of any birds. But suddenly I felt the presence of something unknown to me. Maybe it was the coolness, like a river of air swinging down the mountains or a wave of moist air floating across the savanna. Something was different, but I couldn't pinpoint what it was. I checked the shells in the gun, then quickened my pace, watching every move the dogs made. Close to the bottom of the draw both Shoe and McGillie stopped and half-heartedly pointed under an emery oak and then slowly moved on. I checked under the tree and saw the first signs I believed were quail scratchings. But they seemed so large that I thought they could be wild turkeys.

I knelt down to examine the diggings, but a movement caught my attention. I looked up and McGillie was pointing 50 yards ahead in the bottom of the draw. Shoe was nowhere in sight. I slowly got to my feet and walked toward McGillie, still looking for Shoe, gun ready for a flush of quail. I stopped and slowly scanned both sides of the draw. My eyes focused on a small white spot partly concealed by an evergreen oak. Shoe was also on point halfway up the side of the gradually sloping draw.

I thought, do they both have birds? If McGillie had birds and I shot, Shoe being the older dog may not break his point after the shot. So I decided to stay the course and walk past McGillie. Five or six quail buzzed out from underfoot. I hesitated for a moment, looking at the whole covey. They seemed tail-less, like blunt little rockets. Some were light-colored blurs and others appeared dark. The birds shrieked up the hill toward Shoe. After a foot maneuver around several large boulders, I fired at a light-colored shadow, knocked down the object and it tumbled into a high clump of bunchgrass close to Shoe.

Shoe never moved, but McGillie, in hot pursuit of the downed bird, ran full speed toward his hunting partner, slammed on the brakes less than 10 yards from Shoe, and honored the point.

121

On an adrenaline high, I could feel my heart pounding. I wanted my first Mearns' quail in hand, the one on the ground, before I shot again. But I didn't want to call the dogs off point to find the bird. For me, wingshooting was always this way: every day was exciting and no two days were the same. I looked at the large clump of bunchgrass where the bird lay and then back at Shoe on point.

I was still on a high, walking toward the two dogs on point. I was thinking double, but that was unlikely. Three steps beyond Shoe and the birds went up. Five quail burst out of the cover going in four different directions. I managed to drop the lead bird, then twisted 180 degrees, shot and took leaves out of an emery oak but missed the shot. In a heartbeat, I reloaded and stood waiting for more quail to get up, but nothing happened. My first thought was, "Will I ever have a another chance for a double on Mearns' quail?"

I told the dogs to hunt dead, and in less than a minute McGillie picked up my first bird and placed it in my hand. I was looking at the fat, light-colored hen when McGillie returned with the second bird, a fine rooster. It seemed neither bird had a feather out of place. Looking at this plump-bodied male with its bizarre color pattern, I could see why they were once called harlequin quail, for it looked like a little clown.

I was in a dilemma. I had two coveys scattered and at least 30 minutes to the hunting rig. Daylight was fading fast and time was running out. The wind told me it was still winter, the emery oaks in the mountains were no longer Hooker's green and the shadows on the ground were gone. It was time to turn back. Also, the birds needed to reassemble before the evergreen oaks were black. For me, tomorrow was another day to hunt.

I put the pickup in four-wheel drive, low. We crawled up the steep incline. The rocks looked bigger in the headlights, but the rig came out easily. There was a glow on the horizon. Wilcox, I think.

The Mearns' quail, once called the harlequin or clown quail resembles a comic performer during a pantomime.

KNOWING THE BIRD

Mearns' Quail Origins: In ornithological literature the name is Montezuma quail (*Cyrtonyx montezumae*), named after the last Aztec emperor. The name is appropriate, for this is a majestic, handsome bird. The Montezuma quail has five subspecies, one in the United States and the others found in central and southern Mexico. In most of the birds' range they are called the Montezuma quail, but in the United States the subspecies is called Mearns' quail (*C. m. Mearnsi*), named after Edgar Mearns, a naturalist and U.S. Army doctor who served in the Southwest in the late 1800s.

Before the name Mearns' quail had been adopted, the bird was called the Messena quail. In the mid-1800s the bird was more widespread than today, but due to the great droughts and the arrival of hundreds of herds of livestock on open range this marvelous quail almost vanished in the United States.

In the first half of the last century, the Mearns' quail was quite rare in the U.S. After the decline it was not considered a sporting bird and had no hunting season. Also during this period it was not well known to the outdoorsman, primarily because of its reduced range and solitary life.

Overgrazing and summer drought have always played a part in the fluctuation in yearly numbers, but for the past several decades above-average precipitation and better range management have occurred in some of the Mearns' habitat. If the trend continues, this fine game bird might regain its original historical range.

It was not until the latter half of 20th century that Arizona and New Mexico established hunting seasons for Mearns' quail. Today both states have long Mearns' quail hunting seasons, with generous daily bag limits. Texas has no season. Hunter interest has greatly increased and several thousand Mearns' quail are harvested each year. As a game bird for pointing dogs, this is the bobwhite of the Southwest and one of my favorites.

DISTRIBUTION

The Montezuma quail has a large range. It is essentially a Mexican species, but one of the subspecies, the Mearns' quail, spills over into the United States. The Montezuma quail lives in the regions from central Arizona to central New Mexico, east to central Texas and south to Mexico.

It is a bird of the high savanna, foothills and evergreen mountains of the northern Coahuila, Chihuahua, and the eastern Sonora deserts.

For over a decade I have spent a great deal of time hunting Mearns' quail in Arizona and some in New Mexico. Both states have public areas where one can hunt Mearns', Gambel's and scaled quail. If you are looking for a southwestern Grand Slam, Arizona is the best bet, for it has more available public lands and Indian reservations to hunt.

IN THE BUSH, IN THE HAND

No other species of quail is like the Mearns' in appearance. The male Mearns' quail has brown and black on the back, white polka dotted sides, a rich chocolate belly, jet black legs and a clown-like painted face. The male's wings are grayish brown with white and black marks. The female's pattern is much the same as the male, but the colors are muted. Her facial markings are light brown and pale white. The upper part of her body is almost identical to the male's except that she does not have the grayish tint to her wings.

The Mearns' quail is about the size of the bobwhite. The adult male is about 9 inches in length, has a wingspan of 12 inches and weighs 6 ounces. The female is a bit smaller, but in the hand it appears the same size. Compared to other North American species, the Mearns' quail has a short tail. The sawed-off tail is a good way to identify the bird when it is flying. The Mearns' quail also has the largest and heaviest beak, biggest legs and feet, and the longest claws of any quail. The long, strong legs and large heavy-clawed feet are used to unearth bulbs and other plant roots.

Of all the quail, the Mearns' quail is probably the least vocal, but one call a hunter should know is the assembly call, which is used to reunite the covey. The sound is a series of quavering whistles given by the adults and juveniles of both sexes after the covey has been separated. This shrill call can be heard over 75 yards away. The call is almost mystical but also like it is coming from a comic performer. It has a ventriloquistic quality that makes it extremely difficult to pinpoint. If you imitate this whistle a bird will sometimes answer, helping you approximate its location.

A pair of Mearns' quail may look like a comedy act in a vaudeville show, but when you're hunting them and they flush underfoot, they can make a clown out of you.

Approximate range of the Mearn's quail.

LIFE CYCLE AND BEHAVIOR

In winter, Mearns' quail coveys intermix but do not form large flocks. They are monogamous. The coveys break up in late winter. Pairing begins no later than March, long before a territory is firmly established. Fighting occurs between the males, but whether it is to defend a female or for a territory is uncertain. A male will strut and has a courtship ritual to impress the female, just like other species.

The nesting habits of the three species of quail in the Southwest are quite different and are closely associated to the birds' habitat, terrain, and elevation. Even though there is some overlapping of the species, Gambel's quail live in more arid country, and their nesting period is early and tied more to winter rains in January and February. The summer monsoons do not help them much.

This is not true with scaled and Mearns' quail. In most of their range, both birds live in grassland savanna and higher elevations. The higher elevation allows their nesting to be delayed, making them less dependent on winter rain.

Mearns' quail nesting can begin as early as June and as late as mid-August. This long nesting window is a biological tool for the birds' survival. Simply stated, the time of nesting is determined by summer monsoon rains which produces green foods for adults that trigger nesting instincts and insects for the chicks.

The hen Mearns' quail chooses the bottom of a draw or a low slope with good high cover to build her nest. The nest is on the ground, well constructed and concealed with an overhanging canopy. If the overhead cover is sparse, she will build a cover of dried grass and stems. She is meticulous about lining her nest with leaves, grass, feathers and down. The average clutch is 10 eggs, and the incubation takes about 25 days, which is longer than the other Western quail.

Whether the male helps build the nest is not known, but he does stay close during incubation and will challenge any intruder that threatens the hen. The male also sits on the nest during incubation. It is unknown if the male takes over the duties of the female if she is killed, but all other quail do, so it is very likely a Mearns' quail will do the same. The female will re-nest if the first is lost. Because of delays in the nesting period there is no evidence nor is it likely for her bring off two broods in a single season.

After the last chick is hatched, both parents lead the young away from the nest. The male and female share the duties of caring for the young. Both sexes are very protective and will attempt to lead an intruder away from the brood by pretending to have a broken wing.

Day-old chicks are very active and the principal diet of both the chicks and adults during this time of year is animal matter of many kinds. The adults use calls to keep the chicks together and to alert them to danger.

Young birds develop strong legs at an early age and start to dig and scratch for bulbs and roots. Young birds can fly within two weeks of hatching and become more independent throughout the summer. Adults are very attentive to the young. Family bonding is tight. Even though there is some mixing of others birds, the covey stays together until spring breakup.

The Mearns' quail is a terrestrial bird, preferring to get from place to place by walking, and usually slowly. Even though the birds are capable of moving on the ground fairly quickly, they will fly if disturbed. The birds' flight is not always short. When flushed, the covey splits up, usually flying in one general direction toward a safe escape route.

HABITAT

The home range of the Mearns' quail is as beautiful as the bird. It lives in rolling hills, mountains, deep canyons, steep slopes and rocky ravines. Mearns' quail are seldom found below 3,800 feet and often as high 9,000 feet, with most birds located between 4,000 and 5,500 feet. Typical Mearns' quail habitat is open woodlands and savannas populated by several types of evergreen oaks.

The most important element of the Mearns' quail habitat is not so much the overhead canopy, but adequate understory of a wide variety of bunchgrasses and forbs. The link between summer rainfall and grasses for food and cover is essential for a healthy population.

Studies show that covey numbers and covey sizes are smaller following years with less rainfall. Multiple drought years can have a devastating affect on Mearns' quail populations. When above-average rainfall occurs over several years Mearns' quail can flourish in fringe areas of riparian communities and semi-desert grasslands. I have found Mearns' quail a long way from evergreen oaks forest, even though we think of them as birds of that ecosystem. They are also associated with evergreen oak savanna, but the oak savanna has to have limited or no grazing of livestock with numerous varieties of bunchgrass and forbs to provide food.

The effect of overgrazing on Mearns' quail populations, especially during dry years, has long been recognized. Since southwestern oak savanna is some of the best country for cattle, heavy overgrazing undoubtedly has had a great impact upon the Mearns' quail range. Thick grass, especially bunchgrass, is essential to Mearns' quail for food, cover, roosting and concealment from predation. Overgrazed areas will not hold birds and are not worth hunting.

In Mearns' quail habitat, freezing temperatures do occur during the night but not often during the day. Snowfall also occurs, but this has little affect on the birds' daily lives because the snow that accumulates will melt in a few days.

Mearns' quail range can overlap that of the scaled quail in savanna habitat and the lower foothills of the mountains. I have also found Gambel's quail in the lower arid washes, within sight of Mearns' quail habitat.

FOOD AND WATER

Mearns' quail are ground feeders with strong legs and claws longer than their toes, which are used for digging and scratching. Although insects are taken when available, the predominant diet of the Mearns' quail is bulbs, tubers, mast crops and a great variety of forbs and seeds. The covey travels close together in search of food, raking the understory beneath bushes and trees. These fan-shaped "diggings" can be very large and are easy to identify. Searching will tell you birds are in an area, and where they have been, but finding the birds can be more difficult.

In the late fall and winter, during the hunting season, the crops of Mearns' quail that I have examined mostly contain bulbs and tubers, many being wood sorrel and sedge. In good years of mast crops, acorns from oaks are eaten in great numbers. I have also found insects and seeds in the birds crop during the hunting season.

Open water is used when convenient, but Mearns' quail do not seek out or travel daily to free water. The kinds of food eaten throughout the year supply the birds with their daily moisture requirements. If water is present in the vicinity where I'm hunting Mearns quail, I make a point to look for quail tracks, feathers, diggings and dropping, and many times it has been helpful in finding a covey of quail.

DAILY ROUTINE

There is no need to hunt Mearns' quail early in the morning. Scenting conditions become more favorable for a pointing dog when the birds start moving than when they're tucked under a grassy roost site. They are not early risers, and feeding begins after the sun clears the high hills or mountains. Foraging continues throughout the morning, usually uphill, with a midday rest period. Early afternoon, long before the sun sets, the birds work their way back downhill toward a roost site on the ground. I believe the best time of day to hunt the quail of the evergreen oaks is after 10 o'clock in the morning. A new roost site is selected each evening, usually in the same vicinity as the night before. Tall grass in canyon bottoms and deep draws are preferred roosting places during the summer and fall. During cold winter nights, Mearns' quail roost on grassy hillsides with a southern exposure. For protection, Mearns' quail roost much like bobwhite, huddling together, each facing outward in a circle. While hunting, look for grass that is matted in areas birds may roost. A ring of droppings is easy to see.

I had the first glimpse of this quail one January day many years ago. I'd been on my way to hunt Gambel's quail.

Each step your heart beats a little faster.
Gerald Malzac is about to flush a covey of Mearn's quail.

It was hot, the country arid for miles, and the dogs needed to get out of their crates for a short run. I had been looking quite some time for a good place to stop. The landscape started to change and a National Forest Service sign came into view. At the first gravel road I turned off the highway to exercise the dogs. I drove for about a mile and turned into an unused makeshift deer hunter's camp and stopped when I saw a small bunch of birds on the ground 20 yards in front of me. With binoculars I watched six Mearns' quail dusting in a dry, sandy opening on a trail. Several minutes passed before I got out of the pickup. When I did, they did not flush, but froze. I almost stepped on one bird before it flushed. The others ran under a large manzanita bush. I finally flushed the rest of the covey. I can see why the common name among settlers was the "fool quail." Needless to say, on my way back home I hunted that National Forest for Mearns' quail.

HUNTING MEARNS' QUAIL

Judging from many bird hunters' point of view, the bobwhite is still king of the upland game birds and is high on their wingshooting list. They reason that the bobwhite quail meets all the requirements for hunting with both man and dog. If the bobwhite quail is king in the East, then the Mearns' quail should be the king of the Southwest, for the Mearns' quail has all the attributes of its cousin the bobwhite quail. I believe no other species surpasses its sporting qualities. Like bobwhite, it's a bird for pointing dogs.

In my hunting experiences, Mearns' quail lie better for a pointing dog than any other North American species. A covey of Mearns' quail reacts to danger much like woodcock, by "freezing," spreading themselves as flat as possible and remaining completely still when approached. The male and female Mearns' quail blend perfectly with their surroundings and are much harder to see than a woodcock in its environment.

Mearns' quail have the strongest and largest leg muscles of any quail and prefer to walk or run rather than fly, but the bird will usually run only a short distance if pursued before hiding in grassy cover or flushing. Most game birds that live in the forest under a canopy of trees depend on the understory for concealment, but not Mearns' quail. They either run for cover or freeze, and will never fly into a tree.

This propensity for freezing and hunkering down can

*Little Winston makes a tough retrieve down a steep canyon to put a
beautiful Mearn's quail in Seth Hadley's hand.*

be daunting for a hunter and his dog. Many times I've had my dogs point in an open patch of ground, an act that would usually be considered a false point, but not with Mearns'. There have been times I've encountered this situation and have walked back and forth amongst a covey and finally had the birds flush. It is for this reason a hunter must use a dog. Without one a covey may sit so tight a hunter can pass within inches and not disturb the birds.

Some hunters prefer a close-working pointing dog for hunting Mearns' quail. Their reasoning is to cover a small area thoroughly before moving on. In heavy grass Mearns' quail lie tight. The scent does not permeate the air and the birds can be passed over easily. I prefer to use more than one dog and cover a lot of country and my dogs find their share of birds. Because of the uneven terrain, I use beeper collars on the dogs to locate them. However, like hunting any game bird, I believe the selection of a close working or wide running dog is a personal choice. For Mearns' quail hunting, any pointing dog is better than none.

A covey of Mearns' quail usually scatters when flushed, but travels in one general direction. They're fast flyers with extremely rapid wing beats and they can fly through an oak woods with ease. Mearns' quail do not fly long distances, but on occasion I have seen them travel over 200 yards in open habitat. Their flight is not erratic, but when landing they drop back to the ground, almost free-falling, and use their stout legs to race off and hide.

After landing, a bird runs to the heaviest grass cover available to hide. When this occurs, if a hunter is without a pointing dog, a scattered covey will prove almost impossible to relocate. A good dog with a keen nose that likes to work singles is ideal and the same goes for locating downed birds.

Most of the evergreen oaks grow on north- and east-facing slopes. They are a good place to concentrate when hunting, but later in the day, birds move up the slopes and roost on the south- and west-facing sides where the last sun warms the ground.

Mearns' quail hunting is challenging. As a game bird it's certainly a great bird and high on my list, for it takes me to places that seem mystical. If you're planning a hunting trip to the Southwest, I suggest hunting all three species of Western quail in that area — Gambel's quail, scaled quail and Mearns' quail. If you are unfamiliar with the region, I recommend Arizona because there are lots of public lands available to hunt.

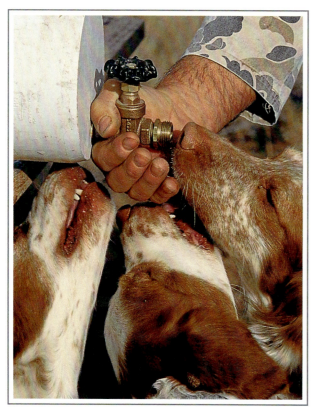

MEARNS' QUAIL

BIRD OF THE EVERGREEN OAKS

Double guns, light loads, pointing dogs, evergreen oaks and Mearns' quail go together. Like their Eastern cousin, the bobwhite quail, they're a gentleman's bird.

I shot a double on Mearns' quail once, but on that covey rise any novice hunter could have done the same. Two dogs were pointing in a creek bottom toward a large clump of rabbit brush. I walked in and the birds flew out as if they were in no hurry to leave. Normally, that's not their behavior and shooting a double can be difficult.

We crossed the sandy bottom and walked through the parched rabbitbrush-covered arroyo. A chain of puddles looked like emeralds lining the creek. The three Brittanys lay, bellies flat, in the crystal-clear water, their first since leaving the pickup truck. Rain hadn't connected the emerald pools for several weeks and the rabbitbrush had lost its tint of pale green. Only the thick leaves of the evergreen oaks held their color.

Seth Hadley followed the dogs, turning up the steep canyon that funneled into the arroyo. I walked a rocky, well-used deer trail that paralleled the canyon floor. Emery oaks, bunchgrass, and rocky outcroppings made up the landscape on both sides of the canyon, which stretched the limits of the eye. Heat waves danced above the rocks. The wind that usually beats the mountains had not stirred the leaves and the only sound was the three dog beepers deep within the canyon giving me Seth's approximate position among the evergreen oaks. Acorns covered the ground under the trees and the quail could be feeding anywhere.

The trail led me higher toward a mountain ridge, away from the canyon. A single shot rang out below and moments later three Mearns' quail flew toward me and disappeared into the oaks before I had my gun up. One dog followed in the direction of the birds' flight path and the sound of the beeper faded into the forest.

Seth worked his way up the steep hill and presented me with a fistful of light buff feathers. A beautiful Mearns quail hen lay in his hand. He slipped the quail into his vest and asked if I had seen any of the covey. We climbed the hillside where I thought the birds may have landed, but the three Brittanys seemed uninterested in my proposed location. They searched the area thoroughly but found no birds.

Seth had found a small pocket of water not far from where he had flushed the covey of birds in the bottom of the canyon. We worked our way back down to the canyon floor. The dished-out sandstone rock formation, eroded over eons, was a good watering hole for the dogs and a great place to have lunch out of the hot noonday sun.

The dogs were lying under a overhanging tree limb, their wet bellies darkening the sandstone, when we heard the call of a Mearns' quail not far from where I thought the birds had landed. The dogs heard the sound too and scurried up the hill in the direction of the sound.

After a long hike back up the hill, Seth and I moved toward the sound of the beepers. One dog was locked up on point in the opposite direction farther away than the other two motionless Brittanys. I walked toward the single dog; Seth went toward the brace of dogs. Both birds seemed to flush and feather the wind at the same moment. Seth's fine rooster tumbled to the ground after the shot; mine dodged around a large emery oak, my slow swing cutting a hole through the lower branches. As we walked back to the pickup, I thought about this magnificent, solitary, high, arid country. To me, the emery oaks, the tall bunchgrass and the Mearns' quail are offspring of the wind, as I believe are the whispering piney woods and the bobwhite quail.

BIRD OF THE OAK SAVANNA

Evergreen oak savannas commonly occur in the higher foothills of the southwestern United States and northern Mexico. The most common tree is the emery oak. As foothills give way to the mountains, the landscape changes from savanna to forest. My good friend Gerald Malzac suggested I hunt both of them for Mearns' quail. He is a building contractor, but my affiliation with him is as an outdoorsman, a keen deer hunter and a self-taught field biologist who knows the flora and fauna from the arid desert floor to the tops of the mountain of the southwest. He told me to look for the pointleaf manzanita bush when driving the foothills towards the mountains. It's a indicator plant that shows the best elevations to hunt Mearns' quail. Not only the evergreen oak, but also the manzanita bush, is a gauge for hunting Mearns' quail.

The jumping cholla stands tall, its many arms ready to do battle with any intruder. Beneath the cholla the grassy bunchgrass understory lays silent, waiting to flow with the first breath of air. This expansive cholla domain is home to the scaled quail.

My three dogs worked the large plain, gingerly weaving through the tall cholla sentinels towards the canyon.

Bottoms of draws sometimes hold little pools of water, good places for
Mearn's quail, but also for the dog to take a rest.

I passed the large reservoir. The dogs ran the eastern slope of the rocky canyon. A month ago, Gerald flushed two coveys of Mearns' quail in the long canyon, which dumps the monsoon rains into the water hole. Coming off the mountain, he'd been looking for a big buck that hangs out with a small herd of does above the reservoir.

Mesquite thickets, junipers and other woody cover encompass the reservoir and are scattered throughout the wide canyon. Several large coveys of Gambel's quail use the surrounding area and venture into the cholla landscape. I didn't realize that above the large watering hole there were Mearns quail, until Gerald told me.

The dogs took a side draw leading away from the main canyon. I followed and angled up the steep side, then walked the ridge toward the higher hills. Manzanita bushes dotted both sides of the ridge. Above, evergreen oaks hugged the contour and lined the sky. High above the field of cholla, I stopped to rest. The reservoir was a silver coin in a sea of muted greens and browns.

Time passed, and for a few minutes I was wondering about the habitat. I knew that the most favorable habitat for Mearns' quail has a canopy of oak trees covering at least 25 percent of the landscape, but I have found them in a lot less cover. I hunt many of these out-of-the-way places every year

and the amount of summer moisture does not seem to be a factor. The elevations at which I hunt are all above 4,000 feet, but I believe the reason these areas have Mearns' quail is that they have optimal food, tall bunchgrass cover and no grazing.

The dogs returned to where I was sitting. They seemed to think I should be on my way. There was more to the upper canyon than seen from below. I worked my way down, starting at the head of the next draw that leads back to the main canyon. After 50 yards the draw deepend and on one side a rocky outcropping formed a straight wall. The opposite side was a steep, grassy slope. The bottom of the draw was wide with a golden stream of bunchgrass flowing slowly downward around mounds of sandstone.

The three dogs came thundering over the ridge and rushed down the steep slope into the bottom. I stayed on the crest of the draw, watching the dogs fan out and work the grassy bottom. Winston was first to stop, then Hershey, then Mac. I scurried down halfway, stopped and waited for the flush. I moved again in front of Winston. I had got them, I was sure. The birds flushed. The second covey the dogs found after lunch.

One or two coveys seem to be there every year. I usually find them where the pointleaf manzanita bushes start in sight of the evergreen oaks.

BIRD OF THE RIPARIAN WASH

In consecutive years of good moisture, Mearns' quail can be far from the evergreen woods. What comes to mind as I drive away from the dark green mountains is a blend of colors in muted shades of yellow, green and brown. The pickup follows the contours of the rolling hills covered with oaks, then juniper, yucca, catclaw and cholla. We pass through a large flat, now a dry lake bed that was once a large body of water before the mountains were formed. This subtle landscape is blue grama grass, mesquite, reservoirs and stock tanks. Farther on, the country changes as we travel along a tree-lined draw, driving through creosote brush, rubber rabbitbrush that has its own distinct and pungent scent. We cross a dry wash and several kinds of ducks wing off the ponds alongside the gravel road. I stop and park under a large willow. Our destination is a riparian community. This is where Tom Petrie and I both shot a hen and rooster Mearns' quail and collected a Grand Slam that day.

Chapter Six
MOUNTAIN QUAIL

Mountain quail can be puzzling and difficult to hunt.

Idaho: Apparently they were going to water after their morning feed. Before driving on to Lewiston, Idaho, then home, I took a water walk along the Little Salmon River. Two adult mountain quail with six young were gathered around a small puddle of water. I got within 20 feet before they ran to heavy cover. Since then, I have found it is not uncommon to get very close to them before they show any sign of alarm.

Leavenworth, Washington, doesn't have a true sunrise — the sun appears suddenly over the high mountains. The Wenatchee Hills humped up in the back window on the blue Volkswagen. They loomed dry in the heat of late fall. I crossed the water that drains the Okanogan Valley and slowly climbed out of the Columbia River's basalt gorge. Then the true sunrise emerged and back-lit the grain elevators of Waterville.

Driving, I wiped off the windshield, but streaks never disappeared until the sun was higher. Gina and Lola were curled up in the back window well of the Volkswagen. Coffee sounded good, so I filled the plastic Thermos cup with one hand, holding the other on the wheel, watching the cut wheat fields swirl by.

Coulee City was a bit out of the way, but that was where I was meeting my hunting partner, Randy. He's a basketball and football coach in a class C school. It was in between seasons, so with a few days off we decided to go bird hunting—our first for mountain quail.

Randy's a big, tall, lean guy. He played basketball for a collage in Ellensburg. He's in his early 30s and has lived in Washington all his life. He's never married, but is looking when he is not playing baseball, basketball, fishing or big game hunting. He and I spend a lot of time fly-fishing the potholes below O'Sullivan Dam of the Potholes Reservoir. He took up bird hunting after he met me. He doesn't have a bird dog, but is seriously thinking of getting one. His real passion is mule deer hunting in the open sage brush country in eastern Washington.

I was following the black highway to Moses Lake. Randy was looking out the window for big game even though the season was over. He's always talking about big horns. Randy's main goal in life is to get a trophy mule deer in the Boone and Crockett Record Book.

Moses Lake is halfway to the Blue Mountains in the Umatilla National Forest, but the wildlife biologist told me it's the best place in the state to hunt mountain quail. The Blue Mountains are dryer and the country more open than the coastal range.

The cafe had no name until years later when the interstate highway went through, but the name "Mom's" never helped business because the freeway was too far. Small town cafes and hotels even then were a dying breed. Barber shops in large towns were the men's gossip page. In many small towns across the prairie states, cafes and bars were in the same location or partitioned off, with an inside door between them. Depending on the time of day, one or the other was used as the information center, from gospel to gossip and births to burials.

Looking out the front window, painted on the inside on the plate glass is "raB dna efaC s'moM." I was finishing a fine chicken fried steak with mashed potatoes and gravy. Randy has a hamburger and fries. I looked at a sign above the chalkboard menu, "T bones 1 buck, with meat 4 bucks," then at the menu. Written in permanent white paint at the bottom was "Mom's Homemade Pie, Today." "Apple Cream" was written in chalk. I ask the waitress what apple cream is.

"I'm new here, I'll ask." She called to the kitchen, "What's apple cream?"

Someone called out from the kitchen, "It's just apple, no one erased the cream."

We both ordered the apple. The waitress called out to the kitchen again, "Two apples."

From the kitchen we head, "Only one apple left, but have a slice of Banana Cream from yesterday."

Randy and I shared the apple pie. Two men from the men's table were watching us. (Women are not allowed at the men's table.) They were looking at us like we were different. I slid the dish of pie back to Randy and told him to keep it.

The waitress handed me the check and said, "The pie is on the house because we only had one piece left." I thanked her and gave her five bucks — enough for the two meals and a fifty-cent tip.

Years ago, I was thinking about buying a house in a small town for a place to stay while bird hunting. It was a great little town, wrapped in sagebrush and it had excellent hunting. My friend, John, a rancher, lived close to town. He called and informed me there was a house for sale — a fixer-upper, for less than $4,000. It was listed (by word of mouth) with a realtor who sold large ranches and happened to live in town.

I called and made an appointment. The time and meeting place was at noon in the town cafe and bar owned by his wife. The place was packed, but the realtor was holding a table for us. Everyone in the place knew John and the realtor. Looking around, I recognized no one, nor did they know me, except that I looked the part of a perspective buyer.

The waitress took our order. The small cafe held twelve tables and the backs of the chairs touch. Coffee poured, the topic of discussion at our table was the house for sale in town. Throughout the meal, no one seemed in a hurry to leave and the premises were unusually quiet. I had just finished a wonderful half-pound hamburger with fries when a women in her early 40s came over and said hello to John and the realtor, then introduced herself to me.

"I overheard your conversation," she said, "about the house in town. My house is for sale." John looked at her and laughed. "Mabel," he said, "he's looking for house, not a cook." She laughed and so did everyone else in the cafe. She called across the cafe to the waitress, "Bring these guys more coffee." The place began to clear out.

John Nash's two English setters have a covey of mountain quail pinned down not far off the two rut road.

There are days I wish I had bought that house. Today, small town mom and pop cafes are few. They are pleasant places to have a coffee in a porcelain cup, a burger made from real beef and listen to stories of local events.

It was early afternoon and we were taking every back-county blacktop road trying to cut the distance to our destination. The western hills had blocked the last rays of sunlight. Setting up camp in semi-darkness is no fun.

I was sitting on sixty years of annual rings, a Ponderosa pine stump, throwing pine needles in a small wood fire. The two Brittanys were at my feet. Randy was cleaning the mess kit in a feeder stream next to our makeshift camp. The forest was asleep. I zipped the Thermos Pop Tent's canvas door closed and the four of us turned in for the night.

We slept past 7 o'clock, then the two dogs got me up, growling at a raccoon or something outside. Coffee brewing, I said to Randy, "Today we have our work cut out for us trying to find birds. All I know about this place is the north slope of the Blue Mountains is supposed to have mountain quail."

Randy and I decided to split up and meet every hour or so. If we saw birds we'd fire a shot to signal the other person. The more ground covered, the better the chances of finding a covey. I suggested we search the edges around heavy cover and dirt roads for tracks and listen for birds calling. I figured most of the things that work for hunting other game birds would work for mountain quail. I did know mountain quail rarely get far from dense overheard cover and they like to be close to water.

As I walked an old logging road, I kept telling myself to stay alert, look for water and watch the edges of the cover. I kept my eyes focused on the dogs, but they seemed to have no interest in getting off the dusty road. I walked uphill for several miles, looking down into a heavily wooded draw. The road became a trail, then abruptly ended at a washed-out landslide. The dogs returned from the bottom of the draw dry and hot. I gave them each a drink of water from my canteen, turned around and backtracked.

As I walked toward the western horizon it was a windless, cloudless day. Far below were pale yellow and gray-black fields. The alternating colors followed the contour of the rolling landscape. Red and white buildings marked the homesteads. From up here, they all looked the same and were boxed in by trees, windbreaks that stopped the blowing soil and winter snows. Far off it looked like Park Place and Baltic Avenue, then I passed "Go." Someone had a row of hotels, not square red blocks, but tall round steel cylinders. I thought that person must be winning!

When one hunts mountain quail it seems all trails lead up.

The plan was to return in an hour, but that never seems to work. Neither of us found any birds.

After lunch, Randy and I spent the rest of the day together, walking trails, burnouts and old roads not traveled by vehicles for years. Later, we stepped into the Volkswagen, tired and hungry. The dogs in the back seat seemed tired, too. I asked Randy what he would like for supper, hot dogs and beans or hamburgers and beans. He laughed and said, "What we don't have tonight we will have tomorrow."

The next morning I rose long before the sun bursts over the mountains. The Wenaha Tucannon Wilderness loomed above me big, rugged and majestic. It's part of the Blue Mountain chain of the Umatilla National Forest. Lying between southeastern Washington and northeastern Oregon, they are a massive range that extends over 100 miles and stops abruptly at rivers at both ends. The Blues are the birthplace and headwaters of many streams and rivers such as the John Day and Grande Ronde. Some flow into the Snake River, others into the Columbia River, but eventually all the water dumps into the Columbia and the Pacific Ocean. Steelhead spawn in the shadows of the Blue Mountains.

Holding a hot tin cup of coffee and waiting for Randy and the dogs to come out of the tent, I followed rivers with a pencil on a map to see how far the steelhead makes its run.

The fish swim hundreds of miles and ascend fish ladders over the dams of the Columbia and Snake and finally travel the clear, cold water of the Grande Ronde to bring new life to the mountains. "Damn those dams," for holding back those silver streaks, I said to myself.

Steelhead are sea-run rainbow trout with big shoulders that spawn in fresh water streams. Steelhead are just that, made of steel — wild, hard and fighting every inch of tumbling mountain water to reach their goal.

Conditions have to be right to find them, but they are worth chasing from the mouths to the headwaters of rivers that hold them. Of all fly fishing, steelhead fishing seems to run in my blood. Thinking steelhead, I wondered if mountain quail are the steelhead of the quail family. Sometimes it takes days to hook a steelhead. Maybe it is the same with mountain quail. They're both a species of wild, rugged, mountain country.

First one dogs showed from the tent, then the other, then Randy. I poured him a cup of coffee and said, "Let's go steelheading." He looked at me, never saying a word, took a slug of coffee, filled a wash basin with cold water from the plastic bucket and washed his face. I explained my steelhead, mountain quail theory. Randy dried his face and shook his head in agreement.

We drove miles of mountain roads, stopping at every draw that looked good for quail. The dogs worked the slopes and ridges, but found no sign of birds. We hunted hard all morning. The dogs hung around patiently while we ate lunch — if you can call an orange lunch.

I said to Randy, "Maybe mountain quail are more like steelhead than I think. Perhaps it's more luck than skill. I wonder if they move like steelhead."

Randy responded, "Ben I don't know anything about these birds."

"Randy, I have read mountain quail that live in the Sierra Nevada Mountains migrate down from higher elevations after a snowfall. I know there is no snow here, but that gives me an idea. Maybe we are hunting too high even though this is the area the biologist said he saw quail. We haven't found any birds so what do you think about moving lower?"

"We've got nothing to lose," Randy answered.

It took almost an hour. We stopped at camp and made a sandwich on the run and ate it on the way down. Coming from Cascade Range below camp the mountains were more like hills to me. The Blue Mountains are a montane forest that lies in the rain shadow of the Cascades and have a lot less precipitation. The forest was open. Ponderosa pine covered the hills. Below, the draws were no longer steep, but thick with woody vegetation. Even though it was much drier, surface water was present and brush covered about half the area. Here I could walk in an opening around the brush, but not in a straight line.

The lower landscape looked different. Here the pale yellow was wheat stubble, plow lines showed in the black fallow fields and most of the red and white buildings were blocked from view by the hills.

For at least two miles Randy and I hunted a brushy draw that lead out of the National Forest into an open hilly prairie. We stopped and moved to the next draw, slowly working back toward the Volkswagen. Within minutes the brushy draw thickened and hiking became slow.

At the top of the draw, I arrived at an overgrown logging road, the sun low on my back. The dogs were walking along side when Randy broke through the heavy cover onto the road. Shaded from the setting sun, the four of us followed the rocky dirt road toward the vehicle. The road became steep, and we were still another 10 or 20 minutes away from where I parked. The two dogs heard the hissing water first and ran ahead.

When we arrived, the dogs were lying belly deep in a muddy pool in the road. A small stream poured out of a steep rocky hillside above us, spattering water on the road and over the other side. Below the road, the slope was gradual. The water had cut its way through the open forest of grass, brush and small trees. Far below was a pond surround by bush. It was a hidden oasis that could only be seen from above.

I was watching the dogs in the pool. Randy, being a deer hunter, spotted them first and whispered, "Tracks." Quail tracks! Even in the low light, the tracks could be seen leading up the trail toward our destination. We were both counting out loud, seven, eight, nine. No eight, then the tracks disappeared over the side. "Do you think the quail heard or saw us?" I asked.

"I don't think so. The tracks are not running birds. It looks like the birds were getting a drink and worked their way along the logging road."

"That seems right, Randy, probably drinking water before going to roost. They have to be close by."

On the final day, both of us were up early. We only had a half a day to hunt. I made breakfast, then lunch to eat on the way home. Randy dismantled the camp.

"Randy, I figure the covey will be between the logging road and the pond below. It's 20 minutes from camp to where we parked yesterday and 10 minutes down the logging road to the water hole. By the time we get there the birds should be finished feeding and be close to water."

First things first, we both checked for new tracks around the water hole and along the dirt road but didn't find any new tracks. I explained to Randy that we'd start right here and hunt to the pond below. This may have been a disadvantage for the dogs because the air current is also going downhill. Hopefully the dogs would work back and forth along the slope and point the quail before they ran or flushed. I had read it is better to be above the birds because they will not run downhill. They will either run along the slope or flush. The first thing is to break them up, then the singles should hold for the dogs.

I walked down the gentle slope. Gina, the better of my two dogs, worked methodically in front of me. She worked the wind current, running down 50 to 60 yards, then hunting back toward me. Lola was hunting off to the side and seemed to be more interested in looking in gopher holes than for hunting birds.

Mountain quail are the largest of the North American quails, and appear to be sentinels of the forest.

Farther along, the terrain became hilly but was still a gradual slope. Half the land was covered with high bush and trees, but with little understory. There was no pattern to the bush and I wove through the opening of short mix grass, snowberry and other low shrubs. I couldn't see Randy, but I could hear him off to my right, breaking brush. The pond was no longer visible but close by, a quarter of a mile at most.

Here the country was rolling, with more draws, but I was losing less elevation. I could see the wheatfields below the openings in the hardwood.

"Ben!" Randy yelled, "Both dogs are pointing in the brush across the pond from me. There are tracks all over. If you come toward me, you'll see the two dogs. I'm going to walk around the pond and meet you."

Randy came up and we moved in on the covey under the overhead cover. The birds seemed hypnotized by the dogs. We walked almost to the edge of the brush before the birds exploded in all directions. Both of us shot. Two quail dropped on the other side of the brush, the rest of the covey followed the tree line around the pond. Gina gently placed a mountain quail in my hand, then returned for the other downed bird.

The two birds were beautiful. Both sexes looked the same so we didn't know if the birds were male or female. Randy and I shook hands. While examining the birds, Lola was on the far side of the pond pointing, her head buried in the brush. Both of us hurried over. I said to Randy, "When Lola points something is under her nose."

Minutes later Gina found two more singles. It was fast hunting for the next hour. The dogs found two more coveys within a 100-yard radius of the pond. All in all, it was a fine, rewarding hunt. But I was glad we packed the Volkswagen. It was late afternoon when we drove by the wheatfield that touched the National forest line.

KNOWING THE BIRD

Mountain Quail Origins: The mountain quail (*Oreortyx pictus*) has five recognized subspecies. These subspecies are distributed in different mountain regions of the birds' overall range. The name mountain quail has always been used throughout the birds' range, but they still have a few colloquial names such as mountain partridge, painted quail, plumed quail and San Pedro quail.

Today, even taxonomists disagree about the number of

subspecies, but generally speaking, the northern and coastal mountain quail are darker, with more brown, and southern birds are a bit lighter and have more shades of gray. To the untrained eye these variations in plumage are difficult to distinguish. To confuse the issue of identification further, in areas where mountain and valley quail ranges overlap, birds have been known to hybridize.

It's only been in the last couple of decades that wildlife biologists have taken a great interest in researching the ecology and population dynamics of this species. These recent studies have disclosed new information of the birds' social life and territorial behavior. Research done by wildlife biologists working for state or federal agencies, universities, private institutions and research stations is the foundation for wildlife preservation and for maintaining our hunting heritage. Every dollar spent researching wildlife benefits today's outdoor person and generations to come.

DISTRIBUTION

The mountain quail is a bird of the highlands of far western North America.

It's a quail of the northwest coastal forest, Rocky Mountain montane forests, the Sierran montane forest, and the woodlands and chaparral forests of Washington, Oregon, Idaho, Nevada and California. The birds live in altitudes of 500 feet to as high as 10,000 feet. The bird was introduced into British Columbia, but today the only birds north of Washington state live in southern Vancouver Island, British Columbia. The birds' most southern range is northern Baja, California.

I have hunted mountain quail almost every season and find them interesting, especially with bird dogs. From a hunter's view point, they are the most misunderstood game bird in America.

Over 40 years ago, I started hunting gray partridge in the western United States. Back then I was told they were impossible to hunt with bird dogs and you could not get within shooting distance of them. I proved that wrong. With my limited experience hunting mountain quail, I compared them to Huns, and like Huns I believed hunting mountain quail with dogs in some areas of their range could be outstanding. I was not talking numbers of birds killed—I was talking about quality hunting. I was thinking Sierra Nevada, woodlands, and chaparral country.

Approximate range of mountain quail

IN THE BUSH, IN THE HAND

The mountain hiker may know and then hear a high, clear call from a steep evergreen slope or woodland chaparral. He may even catch a glimpse of this elegant quail from an elevated perch vanishing before his eyes. But the call is heard more than the bird is seen. The most common call in spring is the male's two-note whistle, *quee-ark*, several-second pause, *quee-ark*, several-second pause, *quee-ark*. This can go on for five to 10 minutes with the last note sounding somewhat like a bobwhite. The male lowers its head, throws it backward and makes a loud, clear call that can be heard at a great distance. The male also has a low-pitched call, *took, took, took*, that is used during the breeding season.

Throughout the hunting season, mountain quail are extremely vocal. The assembly call is frequently heard at sunrise and also to gather a covey back together. When hunting listen for these sharp rallying whistles. The *kow, kow, kow, kow, kow, kow* call is often repeated several times.

The mountain quail is the largest of all the quail species in the United States. The male and female are very similar in appearance and in the hand they are almost impossible to tell apart because their coloring is identical.

Both sexes have a long, narrow, straight jet-black plume about two inches in length composed of two long feathers. One slight difference between the sexes is that the hen is a bit smaller and her plume is slightly shorter.

The adult male mountain quail is about 12 inches long, weighs 9 to 10 ounces and has a wingspan of 14 inches. The throat is dark brown with a wide white line that extends from the beak around the eye and follows the sides of the brown patch. The flanks are also a dark brown. There are about eight white, curved bars over the dark brown flanks. The back and tail are olive-brown. A white streak separates the back and flanks. The top of the head, the nape of the neck and the breast are slate-blue gray. The bill and eyes are black and the feet and legs a grayish-black. The most distinguishing marks are the throat and the flanks.

LIFE CYCLE AND BEHAVIOR

Mountain quail never form large coveys, but one or two families and non-breeding adults may come together in the fall forming groups of up to 20 birds. Not all populations of mountain quail make shifts in elevation in fall and winter. Coveys that live below the snow line generally do not move. For upland game birds, I prefer to us the terms "seasonal shifts" or "movements" instead of the word "migration." I think of migration as great distances, and shifts being changes in elevation. Several other game birds make seasonal shifts from summer to winter ranges. Some are only several hundred yards and others many miles.

Like other game birds, the distances of downward movement for mountain quail are not always influenced by the weather and snow depths. Other factors may trigger the birds' movements. Birds that live in areas that receive large amounts of snowfall seem to move longer distances. These downward shifts can be from a few miles to over 20 miles. In some areas, seasonal shifts start as early as mid-August with the first snows. If snow does not come until later, the birds may not leave until later, but by early October most birds have moved. Mountain quail do not move any lower than they have to. Most birds are below 5,000 feet by late fall and can be as low as 500 feet.

In the fall, a covey stays together when moving to lower elevations. There have been sighting that indicate mountain quail use draws and valleys, following good cover when traveling, but this downward movement can take some time.

Mountain quail start pairing in late winter and early spring when they are in their lower elevations. By spring coveys have separated and birds return to higher elevation in singles and pairs. Males begin calling during spring breakup, usually from a high perch. Like other game birds, mountain quail go through a series of breeding rituals. Birds are sexually mature their first year and will breed if conditions are favorable.

The mountain quail nest is scooped out and built on the ground, usually in very dense overhead cover. Many are on steep slopes. Nests are highly concealed and very difficult to locate. The nest is lined with grass, pine needles and other dry vegetation.

The number of eggs in a clutch is between 9 and 14. Incubation is 24 to 25 days. The male stays in the vicinity of the nest during incubation and is alert for any danger to the hen. If the first nest is lost, it is very likely she will set up housekeeping again. Recent studies suggest that in good reproductive years some pairs may double-clutch, the male incubating the first clutch and the female the second.

Mountain quail are no different than their other western cousins. Winter and spring rains strongly influence good or poor reproductive years. Years of high rainfall in especially dry areas assure more birds nesting and greater numbers of young in the fall season. Also more moisture produces more green plants, cover and insects, which are needed for raising the young.

After the chicks have hatched they are led away from the nest. Both parents care for the young. If the male and female each bring off a brood, one adult assumes all the duties of caring for the young. The first day after hatching, the chicks can walk and feed. Within a week young birds can fly short distances. Both parents use a repertoire of calls to communicate with the young. The chicks' activity and mobility develop very rapidly. Like the adults, young birds prefer to run and are reluctant to fly. Young birds always stay close to dense thickets and underbrush. The adults and young usually confine themselves to their own family group during the summer.

HABITAT

Mountain quail are associated with dense, bushy cover. They are birds of mixed evergreen forest, woodland chaparral, edges of mountain meadows and even lofty forested peaks. Habitat of each subspecies can be quite

Some folks think mountain quail are the toughest of the six species in North America to hunt, but it depends on where you find them and the time of year.

different. In some areas the quail live in small, narrow, secluded valleys with free-falling streams. Others live in brushy hills and steep mountain slopes covered with chaparral vegetation, such as snowberry and other hardwoods.

They are also birds of the desert mountains of sage, pinon-juniper, oak vegetation and the high ranges of the Sierra Nevadas. Mountain quail also live in the redwood coastal mountain ranges in humid forest zones with dense undergrowth. In winter they can be found as far down as chemise and greasewood lines.

Mountain quail particularly like areas that have been either timbered off or burned. These areas have abundant re-growth, which provides both food and cover. They are birds of clearings, canyon thickets, and woodland borders near farms.

Good mountain quail cover is sometimes hard to walk through or see over. Mountain quail appear to do best in places where half the area is in brushy cover scattered with evergreens or hardwoods.

One day in the early summer, a day or two after school had gotten out, Brad Williams, a friend and fellow teacher, and I couldn't wait to backpack the Cascade Mountains to

fish. I was armed with 7½ Sila-Flex, Medallion Golden, (MF 75-4 RAF) fly rod, (that's a 4-weight rod today) and Brad with a old 8-foot Heddon bamboo fly rod. We took off before sunup to fish a lake 12 miles into the high mountains.

The 12-mile lake had no bigger cutthroat trout, nor was it any better fishing than 3- or 5-mile lakes, but we were convinced the farther the walk, the bigger the fish. A big cutthroat in that country is 10 to 12 inches, because the high altitude offers little for fish to eat and the growing season is short. But then a 12-inch trout, other than a steelhead, was a big fish to me in those days.

The trail followed a cascading stream to Stuart Lake. When the trail passed close to the stream Brad and I would stop and fish dry flies for small brook trout, in the 5- to 6-inch range. We'd keep some and cook them up for lunch.

Brad went on ahead and I stopped to fish for the third time so we could have six fat little trout apiece. In the Cascade Mountains, leaving a trail and getting to a fast moving stream is an accomplishment in itself. Deadfalls and jackstraw timber cover the forest floor, and I did more climbing than walking to the roaring sound of water. I was looking for pocket water, little bright blue pools the size of a dishpan, to fool another brook trout.

After several casts, I untangled the leader from a fir tree and a loud, high-pitched whistle startled me. A mountain quail wandered out from under a mountain maple across the stream and jumped up on an old cut stump. Occasionally he would pause, stretch out his neck and crow again. Being quite tame, he seemed in no hurry to leave. I watched him for as long as he stayed but I never did see any other birds. They are so striking to see in the wild. Some folks think it is the most beautiful of all the quail. For me that's a hard call. I caught my last brookie for lunch and returned to the trail.

FOOD AND WATER

The diet of mountain quail is similar to that of valley quail, but with the addition of more fruits. More than 80 percent of the quail's diet is made up of vegetable matter. The rest is animal matter such as spiders, beetles, ants and other small insects. Both the adults and young feed on insects. The main foods are seeds, nuts, fruits, flower roots, stalks, stems and leaves of various plants.

In fall and winter when mountain quail move to lower country they will also feed on cultivated grain crops if they're available. Mountain quail have a wide variety of favorite foods, depending on the range in which they live. In some places fruits such as elderberry, serviceberry and grape are eaten. In other locations bullets, acorns and pine nuts are consumed in large quantities.

Mountain quail depend on free water and require a supply more frequently than other western quail. If the amount of water is limited in an area, the birds will probably not be there. Before greens become available, mountain quail are rarely found more than a mile from water and usually much closer. This need is strong enough that during hot weather they will almost always be found within a short distance of open water. Once rains start, birds may move to areas that have new growth on which to feed, but open water is still essential for mountain quail. I believe the most important criteria to look for when hunting mountain quail is water.

DAILY ROUTINE

Some mountain quail roost on the ground, others find a lofty perch in tall woody vegetation to spend the night. Adults brood chicks on the ground when they are very young. As the young birds feather out they roost on the ground or in low limbs. Roost sites are always in dense cover.

Mountain quail are early risers and are feeding by first light. After feeding for several hours they usually go to water. They spend the midday hours loafing and dusting under thick overhead cover. During hot weather birds spend most of the day close to a creek, spring, stream or some water source, but the water has to have good close cover. Birds travel and drink water throughout the day and will do some feeding. By late afternoon the birds return again to their feeding area and forage until dusk, then water again before going to roost.

In late winter, mountain quail feed longer during morning and evening periods because food is more scarce and spread out over a larger area. In lower elevations during the winter, mountain quail roost and loaf under scrub oaks and other similar cover and spend a great deal of time feeding in low brush. They do not move much during this period and will usually be found in the same area they were found previously. At this time of year, it's not uncommon to get very close to them.

HUNTING MOUNTAIN QUAIL

Hunting mountain quail without a dog is tough. Even though it can be done, without a dog it becomes very difficult because they can escape without you being aware they are even around. For the past 50 years I have never hunted without a bird dog and think this fine game bird should be hunted with dogs.

Any breed of dog, whether it's a retriever, flusher or pointer will greatly increase the chance of finding mountain quail. I use the pointing breeds, but that does not mean they are the best choice. Any dog is better than no dog. The greatest advantage of a dog when hunting mountain quail is that they can cover more ground and the dog can work the heavy cover.

The mountain quail is reluctant to fly. It can run very fast and usually has to run only a few steps before it is hidden from sight. When a covey is in dense cover, send the dog after them and break them up. Once flushed and scattered they hold like any other western quail.

The first thing is how to find them. Hunt high ground first and let the dogs work downhill and into the draws. Birds feed and move uphill rather than downhill. When frightened they prefer to race up steep slopes to escape danger. They will not run downhill. This is the time they fly. When birds do flush they never fly very far, but depend on the closest cover to escape. They can reach flight speeds up to 35 miles per hour in a matter of seconds and be out of sight. Finding a downed or crippled bird without a good dog is difficult and you owe it to the bird and yourself not to lose one.

Like hunting any game bird, there are several factors I consider when looking for mountain quail: the time of day, the weather and the habitat. First, the time of day should influence how you hunt an area. If you hunt in the early morning, roosting cover is a good place to start because that's where the birds will most likely be. Coming off the roost, birds leave scent on the ground when going to feed and a bird dog can pick up the trail quite readily.

Later in the morning the quail will be near feeding cover and water. Midday, hunters should focus on dense cover where birds are resting and loafing. Later in the day, hunting should again be centered around good feeding cover.

Even when hunting with dogs, calling to locate a single bird or a covey during the early morning and evening can be very effective. Give the dog a break and sit on a hill or high place and call and listen. Mountain quail often are in very dense cover and when calling, many times you will get a response. Once a covey is scattered birds respond readily to a call. When a covey is found, it will be in the same vicinity on future visits

Mountain quail are not hunted much, but they are an interesting and challenging game bird.

OREGON'S UPLANDS

Oregon has rich and diverse habitats and a wide variety of upland game birds. The Willamette Valley of Oregon is the site of the first successful introduction of ring-necked pheasant in the United States. Today the pheasant is still the most sought after game bird by the residents of the state, but I believe Oregon is best known for its fine Chukar hunting in the dry rimrock country of the state.

The valley quail is an Oregon native and today is among the most widely distributed game bird in the state.

The gray partridge, ruffed grouse, blue grouse, sage grouse, wild turkey and mountain quail also reside in Oregon. Some are native and some have been introduced over the years. One or more species can be found in nearly every part of the state.

I have spent a great deal of time hunting the uplands of Oregon for chukars and valley quail. It has always been productive and I make it a priority to get back at least once each year. But it's only been recently that I have hunted mountain quail in Oregon.

My experiences hunting mountain quail in Oregon have been in the western part of the state. In the coastal range mountain quail thrive in the natural brush lands. This habitat has been created by logging, fire and other disturbances and is very suitable for mountain quail.

Mountain quail coveys in logged-over country are widely separated because all of the country is good bird habitat. So the most popular hunting method and maybe the only way, is to hunt by driving the logging roads until you see birds and then get out and hunt them on foot. Because of the brushy and extremely steep country, the birds have a tendency to run into the heavy cover and disappear. This cover is impregnable and very difficult to hunt.

My friend John Nash, who lives in Roseburg, Oregon, and I hunted mountain quail in the dense forest up in the high ranges of the coastal mountains. John has outstanding English setters and after a short time driving logging roads we discovered this was not the way to hunt these fine birds with dogs. Even though we found birds, the dogs could not work the steep, heavy cover effectively. Both of us felt that road-hunting and bird dogs just don't go together so we gave up.

The next couple of days John and I hunted the foothills of the coastal mountains. The lower country is mixed oak woodland forests, with rolling hills and woody draws with plenty of water.

Crossing the ridge, we began to drop down the rough, rocky road into a brushy canyon. It wasn't long before John's dogs found a covey of mountain quail. The foothills with the high Cascades in the background is one of the most picturesque places I have ever hunted the quail of the mountains.

The foothills of the coastal mountains in Oregon are similar to the lower landscape of places farther south. My next trip for mountain quail was back to the pinon-juniper foothills overlooking the high Sierra Nevada Mountains.

Phil Nash's setter locks up on point in a new growth forest.

SOME THOUGHTS ON HUNTING GEAR

BOOTS ARE MADE FOR WALKING

A man in the army travels on his stomach and his boots. For a bird hunter, boots are the most important.

Writing about gun dogs and game birds is enjoyable, but writing about hunting apparel is about as exciting as cleaning the kennel. Hunters I know just don't talk about clothing very often, but they should, because the right gear can make or break a hunt.

Fly fishermen are different, they take great pride in their uniforms. Like generals in the military or knights in armor, most flyfishers look like they just stepped from the pages of the latest fishing catalog. Fishing rods, reels, lines, glasses, vest, waders, wading boots, hats, and hat pins collected from all over the world are discussed and admired. The contents of a fishing vest are often the center of discussion, for some perhaps more important than the main event of putting a fly on the water.

What do bird hunters carry in their vests? Outside of shotgun shells and dead birds, not much. Bird hunters dress for lots of walking, and so going light is important. Each species of quail lives in different habitat and terrain, so the first consideration for choosing your duds should reflect the type of cover being hunted. Other considerations are climate, season and the weather forecast for the day.

My suggestion for bird hunters' clothing is to first keep it loose for good movement. Don't wear too many layers over your arms; this hampers your gun mount, which can result in poor shooting scores. When it's cold wear a warm vest — perhaps down — which leaves your arms free but doesn't add much bulk. Keeping comfortable while hunting is important, and today's new synthetic materials offer many choices.

One can always borrow clothing. In fact, I keep enough extra clothing in my pickup to outfit a whole gang of unprepared hunters. Footwear, however, should never be loaned to a hunter, even if their size is the same; everyone breaks in footwear differently, and wearing someone else's boots can result in trouble.

Following pointing dogs in big country means walking, so foot care is essential. To me it's most important;

In heavy cover, mountain quail do a lot of running. Phil Nash loses site of a bird in a large slash pile.

footwear can make or break a hunting trip. And remember, one kind of boot isn't always good for all places.

Here's an example: A couple of season ago, I took an inexperienced young man hunting scaled quail in the hilly grasslands. He had soft rubber bottoms and leather tops on his boots. After I told him he might want to rethink his choice in footwear, he scoffed, assuring me his boots could handle any country that we would hunt.

Rubber boots with leather tops are great: I have a pair myself. But I don't use them for hunting all types of terrain. Bobwhites live in different country than scaled quail. After walking through a cholla landscape and climbing steep slopes, he went into town and bought a pair of leather boots. I don't know which was worse, the soft rubber boots or breaking in a new pair. His hunting trip ended earlier than planned with blisters and sore feet.

Good boots are going to cost some money, but they'll last a lot longer than a cheap pair. An avid bird hunter should have at least four pairs of boots; one for cold weather — this pair could be an insulated rubber pair or a leather waterproof Gortex boot; one pair for wet weather — this pair could be a rubber-bottom, leather-top boot or a full-rubber boot

(caution should be taken with these boots, as they have little ankle support and are not designed for walking in hilly or steep country). The other two pairs should be full-leather boots, leather lined, such as the legendary Gokey boots with a good hard lug sole for walking in all kinds of terrain. If properly oiled and resoled occasionally, they'll last a lifetime.

Why would I have two pairs of the same boots? One pair is my shoe size. With these I wear one pair of very thin socks and one pair of sweat socks. The other pair of boots is a half-size larger. These I use for cold weather, so I can wear one pair of sweat socks and one pair of heavy wool socks. I'm a firm believer in wearing two pairs of socks. If movement occurs the two socks rub slightly against each other and are less likely to rub the skin. This stops you from getting blisters and also absorbs moisture between the layers.

A special mention here about snake boots. If you're uncomfortable in snake country, wear some kind of protection. This may be in the form of snake-proof boots, snake-proof gaiters, snake-proof chaps or hard plastic leggings, but remember, some of this gear is heavy.

I don't want to make light of rattlesnakes, but whereas I have encountered lots of rattlesnakes in the field, no harm has ever come to any person I've been hunting with, nor have I ever met anyone who has been bitten while bird hunting. Even though 14 of my dogs have been bitten, all have survived. But dogs and snakes are another story.

TROUSERS

The list of different kinds of hunting pants is as long as a tall man's leg. Most trousers seem to be made for comfort or protection, for few have both qualities. The United States has diverse cover, from grassland plains, arid desert, to dense forest. It's possible to hunt quail in grasslands or cut croplands in shorts and not get scratched. It's also true that there are places to hunt the same birds where a machete would be helpful. Light pants or jeans are adequate for warm weather and open country. Heavy canvas, wool or tough briar-resistant trousers are adequate for cool or cold weather and heavy cover.

Today, I don't use any of them! I used to hunt in jeans and many of my hunting partners still do, but I find them much too tight in the legs for comfortable movement when climbing hills or stepping over high brush. Also, tight-fitting pants allow briars to penetrate and scratch the legs. My hunting trousers are loose, even baggy. The front of the legs and seat of the trousers are heavy double-faced cotton. Loose trousers are cool in warm weather, and when it turns cold I wear a pair of synthetic, stretch-cloth longjohns underneath. The light skin-fitting underwear still allows me good movement when walking,

I keep my inseams cut short, about one third up the boot (three inches off the ground). Pants cut short and without cuffs may not be fashionable, but they're cooler, stay cleaner, and you can walk through thick cover much easier. I use the same trousers for wet or snowy weather by slipping on lightweight, waterproof chaps or bibs, depending on the situation.

Hats are a matter of choice. Some days I wear a baseball cap; other days I wear a wide-brimmed hat. A hat provides for your head, but its primary purpose is for shading your eyes. I don't like bright colored hats, but if hunting with several buddies in heavy cover, spotting one another is important and so bright hats make a difference. I do insist on bright-colored hats if members of the hunting party are young, inexperienced, or if I'm unfamiliar with them. Today, baseball-type hats are adjustable so one size fits all; I have a selection in my hunting rig for folks to use.

Whether you hunt in the high mountains of the west, in the piney woods of the south, the desert savannas or croplands in middle America, the point of a dog and a flush of quail gets in your blood.

I consider a lanyard for holding dog accessories as important as my boots. I never go in the field without it. The lanyard holds two whistles, a pair of long forceps, a comb and small scissors—all useful items for dog care in the field.

Every hunter should wear shooting glasses for protection against twigs, blowing dust and stray shot. Glasses are at the top of my list next to my hunting boots. I seem to shoot better wearing glasses. I prefer orange lenses, as they sharpen my vision by collecting light and improving the definition of objects such as a dark bird flying against a dark background.

Finally, shooting gloves will keep your hands protected from briars, and in hot weather they keep salty sweat off a nice gun's metal. In cold weather, a light insulated pair replace the all-leather gloves.

Your experiences may be different, but in a half-century of roaming after birds and dogs, this is how I've chosen to dress for success.

Suggested Reading

The following books are recommended reading for the quail hunter and outdoorsperson. There are many more interesting reference books available about the subject and the author apologizes for the omission of other listings.

Arizona-Sonora Desert Museum. Edited By Phillips, Steven J. and Comus, Patricia Wentworth.

A Natural History of the Sonoran Desert. Tucson: Arizona-Sonora Desert Museum Press, 2000.

Bass, Rick. *Brown Dog of the Yaak.* Minneapolis: Milkweed Editions, 1999.

Bowlen, Bruce. *The Orvis Wing-shooting Handbook: Proven Techniques for Better Shotgunning.* New York: Nick Lyons Books, 1985.

Brown David E. *Arizona Game Birds.* Arizona: The University of Arizona Press, 1989.

Brown, Lauren. *Grasslands: The Audubon Society Nature Guides.* New York: Alfred A. Knopf, Inc. A Chanticleer Press Edition, 1985.

Edminster, Frank C. *American Game Birds of Field and Forest.* New York: Charles Scribner's Sons, 1954.

Fergus, Jim. *Hunter's Road: A Journey with Gun and dog Across the American uplands.*

New York: Henry Holt and Company, 1992.

Hill, Gene. *Shotgunner's Notebook: The advice and reflections of a Wingshooter.* Traverse City: Countrysport Press, 1989.

Huggler, Tom. *Quail Hunting in America.* Harrisburg: Stackpole Books, 1987.

Johnsgard, Paul A. *Grouse and Quails of North America.* Lincoln: University of Nebraska Press, 1973.

Leopold A. Starker. *The California Quail.* Berkeley: University of California Press, 1977.

Leopold, Aldo. *A Sand Country Almanac: and Sketches Here and There.* New York: Oxford University Press, 1987.

Leopold, Aldo. *Game Management.* Madison: The University of Wisconsin Press, 1933, 1961, 1986.

MacMahon, James A. *Deserts: The Audubon Society Nature Guides.* New York: Published by Alfred A. Knopf, Inc. A Chanticleer Press Edition, 1985.

Martin, Alexander C., Zim, Herbert S., Nelson, Arnold L. *American Wildlife and Plants: A Guide To Wildlife Food Habits.* New York: Dover Publications, Inc.

McClaran, Mitchel P. and Van Devender Thomas R. *The Desert Grassland.* Tucson: The University of Arizona Press.

McPherson, Guy R. *Ecology and Management of North American Savannas.* Tucson: The University of Arizona Press, 1997.

Parton, William "Web" S. *Wingshooter's Guide to Arizona: Upland Birds and Waterfowl.* Gallatin Gateway: Wilderness Adventures Press, 1996.

Peterson, Roger Tory. *Peterson Field Guides to Eastern Birds.* Boston: Houghton Mifflin, 1990.

Peterson, Roger Tory. *Peterson Field Guide to Western Birds.* Boston: Houghton Mifflin, 1990.

Roseberry, John L. and Klimstra. Willard D. *Population Ecology of the Bobwhite.* Carbondale: Southern Illinois University Press, 1984.

Rosene, Walter. *The Bobwhite Quail: It's Life and Management.* New Brunswick: Rutgers University Press, 1969.

Smith, Christopher. *A Field Guide to Upland Bird and Waterfowl Identification.* Montana: Wilderness Adventures Press, 2000.

Smith, Steve. *Hunting Upland Gamebirds.* Harrisburg: Stackpole Books, 1987.

Smith, Steve. *Shotgunner: Reflections on Birds, Guns, and Dogs.* Gallatin Gateway: Wilderness Adventures Press, 1995.

Stoddard, Herbert L. *The Bobwhite Quail: Its Habits, Preservation and Increase.* New York: Charles Scribner's Sons, 1946.

Sutton, Ann and Sutton, Myron. Eastern Forests: The Audubon Society Nature Guides. New York: Alfred A. Knopf, Inc. A Chanticleer Press Edition, 1985.

Terres, John K. *The Audubon Society Encyclopedia of North American Birds.* New York: Alfred A. Knopf, Inc. A Chanticleer Press Edition, 1980.

Valdene, Guy de la. *For a Handful of Feathers.* New York: The Atlantic Monthly Press, 1995.

Vance, Joel. *Bobs, Brush, and Brittanies: A long Love affair with Quail Hunting.* New York: Lyons and Burford, publishers, 1997.

Waterman, Charles F. *Hunting upland Birds.* Selma: Countrysport Press, 1972, 1997.

Whitney, Stephen. *Western Forests: The Audubon Society Nature Guides.* New York: Alfred A. Knopf, Inc. A Chanticleer Press Edition, 1985.

Williams Ben O. *Western Wings: Hunting upland birds on the Northern Prairies.* Gallatin Gateway: Wilderness Adventures Press, 1998.

Williams, Ben O. *American Wingshooting: A Twentieth Century Pictorial Saga.* Minocqua: Willow Creek Press, 1998.

C. SMITH